11+ English:

A Parent's Tool Kit

For Olivia and Francis

11+ English:
A Parent's Tool Kit

Katherine Hamlyn

Illustrations by Noëlle Davies-Brock

Lucas Publications

Published by Lucas Publications 2002
Bowland House, West Street, Alresford S24 9AT

ISBN 09532 65935

Typeset by Atha Bellman Associates

Printed and bound in Great Britain
by The Bath Press

Acknowledgements

Thanks for help and test piloting many of the exercises in this book are due to: Chetan Belliappa, Kevin Finlayson, Alastair Graeme, George Khachadourian, Phodios Matheou, Daniel Paulley, Sam Robinson, Jacob Rutherford, Myles Turner, Michael Whipps, Alex Brett, James Evans, Ted Hensman, Matthew Hunter, Jess Lyons, Fran McCormick, Alex Mitchell, Maggie Redelinghuys, Tom Richards, Sam Roach, Jack Taylor, Matthew Thornhill, Miles Bryan, Becky Carter, Gareth Colley, James Elder, Peter Gambrill, William Garrood, Kathryn Gilbert, Susie Hughes, Thomas MacDonald, Michael Magee, Alice Matthews, Karen McVeagh, Freddie Morgan, Jordan Patel, Sam Robins, Naomi Russell, Hannah Sexton, Joe Stedman, Kishn Thandi, Adrian Woo and Tanik Patel who'd have helped if he'd been there – all of The King's School, Rochester, Preparatory School. Thanks to their Head Master, Roger Overend, and the staff for allowing me to appropriate their classes. Further thanks to Henry Fewster and Andrew Simmons. Thanks to the many – too many to name – children who have helped me evolve the practices and techniques in this book over many enjoyable and productive years. A warm thankyou to Helen Carpenter Couchman and Ralph Lucas of the Good Schools Guide for unwavering support. A further thankyou to my editor, Rolla Carpenter Couchman, for a superb job. And a final thankyou to my own family for sustaining – and healthily resisting – my enthusiasm for nurturing first rate English in all our lives!

We'd Love to Hear from You

It would help us a great deal if we knew how you discovered *11+ English: A Parent's Tool Kit.* Also, any and all comments that you have regarding this book would be gratefully received. As the publishers of *The Good Schools Guide*, we are always interested in parents' views on UK schools as well. The easiest way to reach us and comment on either resource is through our websites at: www.11plusEnglish.com *or* www.gsgdirectory.co.uk.

Alternatively do write to us at:
Lucas Publications, 2 Craven Mews, London SW11 5PW.

The publishers are grateful for permission to reproduce the following copyright excerpts in this book:

Excerpt from *The Silver Sword* by Ian Serraillier
Reproduced with permission of Mrs Serraillier

Excerpt from *My Family and Other Animals* by Gerald Durrell
Reproduced by permission of Curtis Brown Group Ltd, London on behalf of the Estate of Gerald Durrell. Copyright Gerald Durrell, 1956.

Excerpt from *Emil and the Detectives* by Erich Kästner
Reproduced by permission of Curtis Brown Group Ltd, London on behalf of the Estate of Erich Kästner. Copyright Erich Kästner, 1959.

Excerpt from *The Hamlyn Book of Dinosaurs* by Michael Benton.
From *The Hamlyn Book of Dinosaurs*, as per the original book.
With permission of Egmont Books Ltd

Excerpt from *The Childhood of Edward Thomas* by Edward Thomas.
Reproduced by permission of Faber and Faber Ltd

Excerpt from *Atlas of Holy Places and Sacred Sites* by Colin Wilson, 1996, pp. 36–7
Reproduced by permission of Dorling Kindersley Ltd

Excerpt from *Gone Bananas*
Article reproduced with permission of National Trust Magazine (Issue Summer 1998)

Foreword

Do any of these sound like your 10–11 year-old?

● he has lots of imagination but can't seem to get it down on paper

● she can't write a good story and punctuate in the same piece

● when given an essay title she sits for ages and can't think of anything to write

● he hates writing stories

● her stories are rather short and babyish

● he knows spellings for tests and lots of rules but his spelling goes haywire when he writes a story

● she has absolutely no idea of writing to a time limit

● she hasn't a clue as to how to set about comprehensions

● his school teaches scanning and skimming but doesn't do formal exercises like comprehensions

● the teacher says he's lovely but she simply hasn't the time to give him the attention he needs

● she's bright, you want to put her in for an exam for an academically selective school but you know her English needs help

If any of these are familiar, you will probably be concerned about your child's transition to Senior school.

Why?

Work at Key Stage Three level, i.e. the first years of Senior school, is more independent, relies on projects, coursework and confident presentation. Standards in English matter – not just in English as a subject on its own – but in all subjects where reading for meaning and written work matter.

You may have an able child and have decided that an academically selective education is what you want for him or her but you are, perhaps, not quite certain how to go about preparing for the exams. Although Heads of such schools frequently tell prospective parents that special preparation for their exams is unnecessary, this is seldom true. It isn't that they are deliberately misleading you. It is simply that, unlike most state-educated children, children from academically selective junior schools or prep schools are systematically prepared for this type of exam. Selective senior schools are usually unhelpful about allowing prospective parents to see past papers or sample papers. You can ask but don't be surprised to be told that they don't 'publish' these.

Needless to say, notwithstanding improvements in the teaching of able children since recent initiatives such as the National Literacy Strategy, state schools do not and, in fact, need not drill children in formal, timed comprehension exercises and essay writing to the level expected in entrance examinations. Consequently, a bright child who loves spending hours writing stories and who may be an avid reader, will be under a major disadvantage against children drilled at selective junior schools when it comes to taking exams under strict time limits, if he or she has not had some preparation and practice beforehand.

This book is packed with practical advice and helps a parent diagnose and then treat individual problems with

English. Not all the exercises or tips will be necessary for each child but all 10–11 year-olds – whatever their ability – will make major improvements in their English if they and their parents make good use of this book. In this book, we follow two children and their parents – Alice and her father, John, and Rajiv and his mother, Jyoti, as they work together to make their English better. Rajiv and Jyoti have decided to try for a place at a selective school and will need some help in preparing for the examination while Alice and John just want to improve Alice's skills in English before she goes to senior school in the autumn.

You and your child can work along with these two pairs and, like them, decide on which aspects of English need some attention. The important thing is to see it, not as a 'do-or-die' enterprise, but as a 'have-a-go' exercise – something useful and productive but also fun. It is decidedly not something which should lead to tensions and tears!

The book is in three parts. The first part gives basic, general advice on how to improve English at this stage – assessment techniques, practical approaches to comprehensions and essay writing, ways of working on basic skills such as spelling and punctuation. Part Two consists of exercises which build on and practise the techniques given in Part One. Part Three consists of formal exercises, an exam paper and guidance and answers to the exercises in all three parts. Finally, there is an Afterword which will help you and your child programme your own scheme of work based on the guidelines in this book. The approach throughout is practical, traditional and accessible. Confident reading and writing in English – no matter what fashionable methods and strategies come and go – still depend on the mastery of basic skills. This book guides you through them all – without stress!

Contents

PART ONE

Before we begin –
a few common worries

One can't teach one's own child

True enough in some cases. If Alice is used to being criticised or found fault with or if she feels under pressure to perform, it probably won't work. Similarly, if John finds he is unable to contain himself if Alice forgets her apostrophes even after he's spent two whole sessions explaining them, then, probably, the ratio of pain to gain will prompt a frenzied call to a tutor who is no relation. This will be more helpful and healthier in the long run! Alice will have to *want* to improve her English and John will need to understand that Alice isn't being obtuse on purpose. She will need to feel that John is *on her side* – that it is a *joint* project and that he is not going to be critical or punishing but understanding, encouraging and rewarding whenever possible. It is hard, sometimes, to remember that children very nearly always *want* to do well – not just to please their parents but for themselves too. **Praise** is probably John and Jyoti's most valuable tool in this respect.

Similarly, Rajiv will have to *want* to go to the school Jyoti has chosen for him and Jyoti will need to appreciate his fear of failure – of letting her and himself down. If, on the other hand, all Rajiv's junior school friends are going to the local comprehensive and he wants to go there too, he may not want to take the exam and he certainly won't want his mum to help him do extra work for it. Consequently, it is vital that the choice of school or schools is – or at least appears to be – a joint one. If Rajiv is obsessed with football and Jyoti's first choice of school only plays rugby, Rajiv won't want to try for it, however many labs or Oxbridge successes it has.

A relaxed approach will achieve far more than an anxious one.

Have a go

A good idea is for John and Jyoti to have a go themselves at the exercises which follow throughout this book. They will have a better idea of the problems and challenges that seemingly simple tasks present if their experience of such things is not 20-odd years old! Collaboration, too, is often the best method – especially in the early stages – and it will do a lot for Alice and Rajiv's attitude if they see that their parents are not just telling but doing too! In general, a 'have-a-go' approach is the right one. A relaxed attitude and a flexibility about what you try, and when and how, is more likely to make for real progress than a shared anxiety about 'success' and a feeling that getting into the one and only school is the be-all and end-all of life as we know it.

There's no time

If Alice and Rajiv want to improve their English then they will, albeit reluctantly, be prepared to give up an hour a week or so of ballet, sea-scouts, *Neighbours* or whatever it is, for a while. Likewise, John and Jyoti will have to find a time that is possible for them. In general, 8.00 p.m. after a long working day, when both child and parent are tired and, possibly, fractious, is not a good idea. First thing in the morning at a weekend is good as is before the evening meal. Obviously, though, this is not possible in many households. The important thing is that it should be a time when there are as few distractions or competing calls on time and minds as possible. A regular time is best and one during which it should be agreed by the rest of the family that parent and child won't be expected to answer the phone or deal with other immediate needs.

When should we start?

Most school entrance exams are in January but you will

need to check this with the school(s) of your choice. If Rajiv is able and has no real problems with writing or formal exercises, starting the previous September and continuing as regularly as possible should be fine. He will need to practise on as many sample papers as possible and, as the date of the exam approaches, he should stick to the allotted time limits. If, on the other hand, he has more fundamental problems with essay writing or with basics such as spelling, punctuation or reading carefully, Jyoti will need to begin much earlier – maybe even a year before the exams.

If John's concern is simply that Alice's English isn't good enough for her to feel confident in a non-selective senior school and he just wants to help her with the basics, the same time scale applies. Either way, don't despair if there seems an awful lot to do. All children, whether coached or not, make huge strides in this year. A $9\frac{1}{2}$ year-old who cannot write a coherent story, spell any but the most basic words, never spells some words the same way twice and is clueless when faced with a simple comprehension exercise, will astound you at $10\frac{1}{2}$ by his quiet command of all these skills, gained simply through being more mature and more focused on what is required. The one thing most likely to inhibit progress is **anxiety** – often transmitted by loving but over-solicitous parents.

Where do we do it?

The kitchen table is fine. Alice's or Rajiv's room is also fine. Anywhere is fine if the T.V. is off and interruptions are minimised. Lessons should be strictly time-limited to an hour. An hour can seem endless if the going is tough but don't be tempted to go over time even if the lesson has flown by. This way, you'll both look forward to the next one.

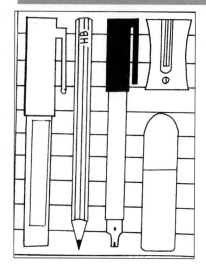

What do we need?

You need an **exercise book**. This, ideally, should be wide-lined with a margin – to save you constantly pencilling them in.

You also need the right writing implement. Schools' practice varies. Some like children to use a **fountain pen** and encourage the use of ink erasers. Others ban these and persist with **pencil** and rubber. Once you have checked whether the school of your choice has a preference, there are only two important factors. The first is **comfort**. A child who is not comfortable holding whatever he writes with will not be at ease with what he writes or the whole business of writing. He will also tire quickly and may develop calluses or blisters on his fingers. A lot of time is wasted in using ink erasers or rubbers. Simple crossing out is the best way to deal with mistakes. Nowadays, cheap **roller pens** are readily available, do not need refilling and produce results as good as fountain pens. The second factor is **legibility**. The most important consideration is that what Rajiv intends to say can be easily read by whoever is marking it. A teacher with 400 scripts to mark won't have the time or patience to decipher Rajiv's writing – however worthy its contents. While many schools – and parents – pay too much attention at this stage to presentation at the expense of content, legibility is crucial.

It is often worth examining a child's **grip** on his writing implement. Some children grip a pencil as though trying to asphyxiate it. Or they may press down too hard on the paper. Sometimes, experimenting with a different hardness of pencil helps this – e.g. substitute a 2B for an HB – the writing will be blacker with far less effort. If Alice is pressing or gripping too hard, suggest that she just *tickles* the page with the point. It is worth spending time practising this. On rare occasions, this can be a symptom of a greater, underlying anxiety which may need investigating. A good

Alexander Technique teacher, with experience in helping children, might be worth consulting but, it should be stressed, this is only very seldom appropriate.

Nearer the time of the exams, Rajiv should practise writing on **A4 lined paper** as this is what most schools will give him to write his exam answers on.

You may find it helpful in the months before you start, to make a collection of **postcards**. These are invaluable as triggers for story writing. Try to make your collection as varied as possible, i.e. landscapes, street scenes, people, abstracts, jokey pictures etc. You can also cut off the pictures from the front of greetings cards and so on but, if you are stuck, then these can, of course, also be found in art shops.

Finally, you will need a **spelling book**. This is normally a very plain address book with indexed pages – preferably with only one letter per page. This is used as your child's personal dictionary and is explained in more detail on pages 53–4. Try to find an address book without too many modern additions such as spaces for email addresses and so on. They are available from stationers but may take some hunting down. The most important thing is that they have enough space – especially if spelling is not your child's strongest point. You'll be amazed how quickly the 's' page, for example, fills up!

Computers

A word about these miraculous and invaluable tools. Most children enjoy doing work on computers and turning out an end product which looks impressive and professional. However, computers are of no help whatsoever when it comes to English skills. Relying on a Spell Check saves the need to learn how to spell – no entrance test, school examination or GCSE in English can yet be taken on a computer (except under very special circumstances, of course). Computers do not

Children need to trust their own spelling skills - no spell checks in exams!

correct 'is' when you meant to write 'in' or 'has' when you want 'was'. There is no substitute for hand writing and eye checking! Consequently, computers are absolutely *out* for the work in this book and, it is to be hoped, for any other work aimed at improving standards and confidence in basic reading and writing skills.

How do we start?

To begin with you will need to make an **assessment**. You may find it helpful to ask a local teacher to help you with this. The ideal person is an experienced Year 6 or Year 7 teacher who should know exactly what the senior school will expect. If you are trying for an academically selective school, the best person would be a teacher familiar with their expectations. Ask around – especially among parents who have been through the process already. Good teachers are well-known in a local area and will be used to making such assessments – of both English and Maths – at this level. However, you may well feel that with a little help you can make such an assessment yourself. You will need to look at how your child tackles **comprehension-type exercises** and **written assignments**. Read on!

Assessment

Comprehensions

Your child may never have heard the word. Whereas most people of his and her parents' or grandparents' generations would have been systematically drilled in this exercise, few children not educated in the more formal, traditional schools still do these exercises – *under that name*. However, if you consult the **National Curriculum for English** or **National Literacy Strategy**, you will find that all the skills associated with comprehensions –

reading for meaning, selecting appropriate material, summarising, recasting in a different form for a specific purpose, giving a personal response and so on – all these vital skills are, and always will be, essential parts of English learning and your child will be acquiring these throughout his or her schooling. For the purposes of this book – which many will use as an aid to preparing for exams which do require comprehension skills and under that name – you can assume that the principal, relevant written skills required to embark on **Key Stage Three English**, i.e. the first years in senior school, are included here under 'Comprehensions' – and a lot more besides!

It is important to know how easily your child understands what he reads. Ask him to fetch one of his books – one, perhaps, he read and enjoyed a year or so ago – which is well within his capacities. Choose a page or so from this book. If he hasn't read one recently – or at all! – pick one of the passages at the end of this book. They have questions appended. Take a minute or two to read through the page you have selected. Then ask him to read it out loud to you. Then ask him some questions – as basic as you like – about what he has read to you. Ideally, these questions will be, firstly, factual – e.g. 'how many children were playing ball/ going fishing/ eating lunch?' or 'what was the name of the man in the shop/ on the boat/ in the prison?' Secondly, ask him questions which require him to make a judgement or give an opinion, e.g. 'why do you think the man wanted to sell his car/ the Headmaster expelled the boy/ the girl was not allowed to go out?' Examples of this kind of question are given after the passages on pages 102–114.

This sort of exercise should help Jyoti determine whether Rajiv grasps what he reads and whether he can express information out loud. If he acquits himself well it is important that he is warmly congratulated and told how clever he is. He may well be nervous at being

A child can find doing schoolwork with a parent confusing at first. Remember - being Mum or Dad comes first!

examined in this way by a parent he is used to seeing in a very different context. If he hasn't done well, it may be that the passage – or the questions – are too difficult, that he is nervous or that he hasn't entirely understood what is required of him. Try again with an easier passage and simpler questions. Don't give too many instructions. The simpler, the better. Children are easily confused or made over-anxious by too many instructions.

Once you have found the right level, practise two or three of these. Then you can move into the first written response to such questions – perhaps only one or two written answers out of five or six questions at first. This will give you an idea of how your child expresses himself on paper – both in terms of his ability to explain or describe things and in terms of his general accuracy. A more detailed approach to comprehension technique is given on pages 24–9 and practice exercises will be found on pages 102–114.

Essay writing

A child given the title 'A Great Day Out' or 'My Worst Nightmare' frequently stares for ages at his page and then, tearfully, confesses, 'I can't think of anything to write.' Conversely, he may smile confidently, begin writing immediately and rapidly and, two lines further on, stop and not know how to continue beyond the first brief inspiration. Other children get excellent ideas but are only just getting into the 'real' story half an hour later when you want them to stop. Cruel though it may seem, for the purposes of timed, assessed, written work, you need to curtail the natural imaginative flow and they need to learn how to control it. John should tell Alice she has exactly half an hour. She can write a story or a description but she must use all her time and get to the end of what she wants to say. John will need to reassure her that the story need not be 'true'. He should stop her after half an hour and then allow her a further five minutes to check very carefully. Then he should suggest she read it aloud to him. This should allow him to assess:

a) whether she can write a connected narrative or description
b) whether she has a sense of writing something for a reader i.e. that a reader can follow and make sense of
c) whether she can punctuate competently
d) whether she can spell most of her words accurately
e) whether she writes interestingly and uses words in a confident, lively and imaginative way
f) whether she has any idea of what writing for half an hour feels like and what can – and can't – be done in that time

The assessment of Alice and Rajiv in all these respects will then help John and Jyoti to judge which sections of this book will be of most use to them. Having read carefully through the rest of Part One, they will then be able to use the Afterword on page 126 to make up their own programme of work.

Now you should have sorted out which aspects of your child's work need help.

Time

A final word, before we start, about the use of time. Rajiv and Alice, whose only experience of tests hitherto may have been SATS, need to understand that they will be given a certain amount of time in an exam and this amount of time is a tool which must be used. This is as true of exams in senior schools as of the entrance tests Rajiv will be taking. There is absolutely no point and no merit in finishing before everyone else. In fact, early finishers probably haven't written enough in either the comprehension exercise or on the essay or both. They must be encouraged to use all the time. Comprehension answers can be made fuller, checked and rechecked.

Essays can be expanded, made clearer, checked and rechecked. As the time of the exams comes closer, Jyoti will need to set time limits for work in order to accustom Rajiv to working within those limits and to completing tasks within them. Gradually, he will begin to *feel* what thirty or forty minutes is like and be able to contain his work within those times. But time wasted will be marks wasted and this is an important idea for him to grasp.

Starting work

Comprehensions

Comprehension means *understanding*. A comprehension exercise is one which tests the child's capacity to read and understand – both the passage set and the questions that follow it. Many children dutifully work through the passage and then skim the questions, answering what they *think* is being asked, rather than making sure they *know* what is being asked. The National Literacy Strategy now teaches skimming and scanning as useful tools – which they are – but they will not do in exercises such as these which depend on an ability to read carefully and *between the lines*! Some children, nervous that they may not manage the questions or the time limits, skim the passage in a quiet panic and then panic even more because, not surprisingly, they don't understand the questions. Some very keen readers do surprisingly poorly on comprehensions, simply because they are used to reading quickly and find it hard to slow down and read sufficiently carefully to take in the necessary detail. It is important to explain to Rajiv and Alice that they will need to read – slowly and meticulously – both the passage and the questions – *as well as any rubric at the head of the paper*. This is an important point as often information about the contents of the passage is given at the top. Missing it out can make understanding the passage far harder!

The passage

Some passages are pretty straightforward and merely require concentration and average intelligence to follow and extract information from. Others require rather more. None should require you to draw on knowledge or information from elsewhere. Therefore, if Rajiv finds himself having to hunt about in his memory for information not in the passage, he has probably misunderstood the question. A passage on dinosaurs, for example, will have in it all the information needed to answer the questions.

Many passages are quite complex and describe a scene in which different people are in different places. An understanding of the passage and, therefore, of the questions, depends on Rajiv being able to use the information given in the passage to picture the scene. Sometimes it even helps to make a rough drawing of who is where! Some passages depend on conversation to create character and atmosphere. Rajiv needs to concentrate on following *who* is speaking and *what* we learn about them from *what* they say and *how* they say it.

Rajiv needs to understand from the outset the importance of reading the passage slowly and carefully. One way of helping him grasp this idea is to explain to him that he needs to be a **detective** to do this work. Hidden in each passage there are clues. He can only find these clues – and therefore solve the questions he will be asked – by reading very, very carefully. There may well be words in the passage that he doesn't know. This is not a calamity – other children won't know them either – but Rajiv needs to learn to use the **context** of the word to try and gauge its meaning – or something close to it. For example, in the sentence, 'It was clear from the *alacrity* with which Patterson entered the room that someone was after him', 'alacrity' – a word which few ten-year-olds would know – could have only a narrow range of meanings in this context. Too long should not be spent on individual words but a sense of the story or meaning of the whole passage is vital. *Time spent on grasping the passage is time saved on decoding the questions.* In other words, if the passage has been understood, then Rajiv should not need to trawl through it again and again for the answer to each new question – though a quick check is reassuring. It is usually a good idea not to read the questions until the passage has been read at least once.

Don't read the questions until you've really grasped the passage.

Comprehension questions
Questions can be purely **factual**, e.g. 'What was the burglar's name?'. They can ask you to **select** material, e.g. 'Which of the animals named in the passage are mammals?' They can ask you to **summarise**, e.g. 'What were Emil's reasons for leaving the train?' They can ask you to make **deductions**, e.g. 'Why do you think the servant felt impatient?' They can also ask you to **develop** ideas or themes contained in the passage or give your own **response**, e.g. 'What do you think happens next?' or 'What do you like about the passage?' Many questions are in two parts and Rajiv needs to be careful to answer the *whole* question – not just the first bit. Many papers specify the number of marks each question is worth. This is a valuable tool. Rajiv needs to understand that it is wasteful to spend ten of the precious forty minutes on a question worth only two marks and, consequently, leave no time for the last question which is worth eight. This involves *looking ahead* and making sure that enough time is left for the most 'valuable' questions.

    Time is of great importance. Most papers are well-constructed and most children will manage to finish – just –

in the allotted time. Occasionally, a paper will be too long and leave children with unanswered questions or, sometimes it will be too short, and children will have unused time at the end. A few basic techniques come in handy.

Full sentences

Some papers specify that complete sentences are required. Others say that they aren't. Either way, it is important that Rajiv knows what this means. This does not mean that a thorough grasp of English grammar, from subjects and predicates through parts of speech to clause analysis is necessary. However, Rajiv will need practice in writing an answer that makes sense as a piece of information, that clearly relates to the passage and could stand on its own. For example, in answer to the question, 'Why do you think Patterson hides under the bed?', 'Because he is scared', would not do but 'Patterson hides because he is scared', would. In general, beginning an answer with 'because' is not a good idea. However, in answer to, 'When Patterson hears the footsteps coming down the long corridor, what does he do?', it is a waste of time to write out all of the information in the question again. 'When he hears the footsteps, he jumps out of the window', is quite sufficient.

These days, many papers require full sentence answers for only some questions and this is made clear. Some questions will need only a one-word answer, e.g. 'What is the man's name?' 'Patterson'. Much time can be wasted on writing out, 'His name is Patterson', when this is not required. The rubric at the top of the paper should make this clear.

Rajiv should be advised to *leave a couple of lines after each answer*. Very often, in the checking time at the end, he may realise that he has answered only half the question or that there is quite a lot more he could say to strengthen his answer. This is much better presented if written on a spare line rather than crammed in over the top or asterisked to elsewhere on the paper.

Finishing early is *not* a good idea. While Rajiv needs to understand that it is important to get moving quickly and not to waste time, the paper is not a race and higher marks are not awarded to those who finish first. Ideally, as we said above, the paper will be so well constructed as to enable good/average candidates to finish in time, just. The vital thing is that if Rajiv finishes early, he does not sit back and watch everyone else write, but that he uses every spare minute he has. Careful checking is vital (see pages 46–52) both of what he has written and of how he has written it.

Points to look for
a) Does my answer make sense?
b) Does it answer the question I was asked?
c) Does it answer the *whole* question I was asked?
d) Is it the same answer as I give to another question? If so, have I understood the questions because no two answers should be the same?
e) Have I left any blanks? It is always better to write *some* kind of answer rather than nothing. A blank space cannot earn any marks. Even a wild guess, though it may not be right, may be partially right and earn a mark or two. A candidate asked to define a word in the passage may not normally have a clue as to what, for example, 'alacrity', means, but should be able to make a guess which may be near enough to earn a mark. *Don't leave gaps!*
f) Have I written enough? If a question is worth 8 marks, it will require a fuller answer than a question worth 2 marks.
g) Are my answers spelled and punctuated correctly? (See pages 46–52 on checking.)

> It is important to use every minute to make the answers as good as possible.

Multiple choice papers

Some schools set a **multiple choice** comprehension paper. These set out the passage in the normal way but follow it with questions where the candidate is offered a choice of answers and has to ring or underline the correct one. There may also be some questions on these papers which require longer, written answers. Rajiv needs to be familiar with this style of paper so as not to be thrown by it. An example is given later in this book and collections of such papers are readily available in shops. Again, it is vital not to leave any question unanswered. Underline or ring *something* for every question!

Essays

Before John begins to work with Alice on stories, a few simple principles will help when it comes to the writing.

A **story** to be written in only 30–60 minutes should have *one* basic idea. Ideally, the action of the story should all be contained in one incident or a brief series of consecutive events. It should have a small number of characters, be in one place, not have chapters, episodes or a series of paragraphs which begin, 'The next day…' or 'Three weeks later…' *The simpler the better*. The reasons for this should be obvious. Complex stories simply don't work in a page or two of writing and won't allow Alice to show how well she writes.

The title

The title is all important. If your title is 'The Whistle' it is no good writing a story about a birthday visit to the zoo and MacDonald's and tagging on a final sentence about how one friend gave you a whistle. Likewise, if the title is 'The Whistle', it equally hopeless to begin: 'Ben was given a beautiful silver whistle for his birthday' and continue with a saga about Ben's visit to the zoo with no further mention of the whistle. Many children lose sight of the title they have been given. This is where a brief plan comes in. (See below!)

Timing

Alice may need a lot of practice in writing to a specific time limit. Perhaps her stories normally fill half an exercise book and take several weeks to finish. She needs to learn what can be accomplished in 30 minutes, 40 minutes, 60 minutes, whilst still coming to a satisfactory conclusion of her story. Simple, containable ideas are, again, vital.

Planning

A story can be like a train journey.

A good analogy is that of a train journey. A train driver leaves his point of departure knowing which stations he must go through in order to reach the final destination. His entire journey is dictated by the movement towards that final destination. If he is not clear what the final destination is, he may well find himself rattling down a branch line or being derailed. It is exactly the same with telling a story. If Alice looks up brightly, fifteen seconds after being given her title and says, 'I've got an idea,' and wants to start writing, she *may* have an entire, complete narrative in her mind. However, she may actually only have the narrative equivalent of the departure platform and no clear idea of where the story is going and what will need to happen on the way to wherever it is heading. Alice will need to spend a few minutes thinking about her story – how *could* it end? What needs to happen to lead up to that end? She could note down a few keywords if that helps. Many children find this idea of thinking ahead a difficult one and for some – the confident, highly imaginative and very organised few – this kind of planning isn't vital. They can get a story back on the rails even from worrying detours into siding sheds. However, for most children, the idea of the train journey, stations *en route* and a final destination, is a great help and cannot be explained and referred to too often. You can also develop it further, e.g. if a new character is to appear, the train needs to stop and pick them up. It is also a way of explaining to Alice how useful description can be (see below). It helps the reader to 'see' what Alice 'sees' on this train journey if some description is included.

If it bores Alice it will bore a reader

What would Alice enjoy reading? If the title is, 'A Party', would she enjoy reading a list-like account of who came, what the presents were, what was eaten, what games were played and so on, if *someone else* had written it? Or would she prefer to read a lively account of who spilled coke over whom, who had a fight, of a very surprising present, an unexpected guest etc? Or would she like to read a story about *preparing* for the party or clearing up afterwards? Both types of story could include lots of detail of the kind Alice would know well through her own experience. The central point here is that Alice needs to imagine her story being read by someone like *her*. What would bore her? What would she herself enjoy reading?

Description, detail and complicated words

'My teacher says I don't get enough description into my stories,' or, 'my teacher says I don't put enough long words into my stories,' (a bit like not taking unnecessary additional vitamins!) Having had this said to them repeatedly, not surprisingly, some children get hung up on 'description'. Description and long words – *for the sake of them* – merely hold up a story and shout out 'artificial!' to any normal reader or examiner. There is no merit in writing 'accustomed to' when 'used to' as in 'Mrs Hobbs was used to cooking a large meal on Thursdays', will do just as well. Meaning can be obscured by the unconfident use of a complex word, when Alice could express herself

Description - with a purpose - makes stories interesting and more fun.

perfectly clearly using straightforward vocabulary with which she is confident.

However, Alice should be encouraged to stretch her own vocabulary – by reading increasingly challenging books and by being helped and encouraged to look up new words in a dictionary whenever appropriate. This way, new words naturally become part of Alice's own vocabulary and will be used unselfconsciously, accurately and in the right places! Description is, of course, an essential part of good writing and detail is essential to description – but it *fulfils a purpose*. It may be necessary to describe a character in the story to help the reader picture what Alice herself imagines him or her to look like. For example: 'Mrs Hobbs, *with her long, sharp chin, splintery teeth and steely voice*, was approaching the classroom…' 'Mrs Hobbs was approaching the classroom…' does not create the same picture at all!

This applies equally to places, weathers, scenes, atmospheres and so on and Alice needs to see the way detail of this kind can help the reader understand what she wants to convey. Practising describing such people, places etc. – independent of story-writing – can be a useful warm-up for the business of making stories later on. She could try writing just a few sentences of description about people she knows – a little exaggeration can come in useful here and there! It is worth repeating though, that the arbitrary inclusion of a paragraph of bored and boring description for the sake of it has no value at all and is not to be encouraged!

Where to start the story?
Few stories need to begin with a detailed account of the main character's parentage, siblings, habitation, neighbours and pets. Alice should see that a story about the arrival of a new teacher in the school need not start as follows: 'My name is Sarah. I live in a house with my

mother and father, my little brother Sam, my hamster, two budgies and my goldfish who is called Goldie...' The important thing is to get to the point. If the story is about a new teacher who is an amazing athlete and who has a habit of standing on his head during lessons or turning mid-air somersaults at unpredictable moments, Alice could begin her story with a group of excited children who have seen a new teacher cartwheeling down the path to the school or with a child turning her head during a lesson and being surprised to see Mr Baggins's heels where she expected his head to be. In other words – *go straight in*. She could even start in the middle and go back to fill in the details, as with the example about Mr Baggins. This technique may be too demanding at first but may be worth playing around with later when a straight line narrative (remember the train!) has been mastered. Flashback techniques, a conversational style and other flexible approaches give a healthy sense of power over their readers that many children, when they are becoming more confident, employ with enthusiasm and enjoyment. Either way, there is no time or justification, in the context of an exam, for preambles. Once Alice knows what her story is about, she should start straight in – and stick to it!

Where to end?

If a story has been properly planned, i.e. Alice knew her destination station before she set out, she will not panic two thirds of the way through, feeling that she has set up a situation that is impossible to resolve and resort to the, 'then Sarah woke up. It had all been a dream!' formula – an escape ending. Neither will she find that the end of her story has lost touch with its beginning and has no relation at all to its title! Ideally, an ending should arise naturally out of the narrative. Sophisticated story-tellers, even at this level, will enjoy confounding the expectations of a

reader. For example, a story called 'The Precious Bowl' which involves Sarah and Laura getting down a precious bowl to put their popcorn in and enjoying an evening's munch in front of the T.V., will not end with the breaking of the bowl but with the breaking of Sarah's leg as Laura knocks her off the chair she is carefully balancing on to replace the bowl. In other words, Alice can have fun confounding the reader's expectations in this way. But this is only for the pros. Less confident writers need help in knowing where to leave their story. Again, the plan – decided before setting out – is helpful but Alice can also be told that it is alright to leave the reader in some doubt about how things would end. Every detail of the characters' future lives needs not be given. Stories can end: '… as we walked back into the classroom, we wondered what on earth Mr Baggins would do next!' or, 'Patterson put the last bullet in his gun. He didn't want to use it but if he had to, he would.' Such endings are dramatic and, though they leave the reader wondering, they are acceptable ways in which to conclude a story.

Where might your story begin? - and end?

Getting started

Possibly the most common response to an essay writing task is, 'I can't think of anything to write'. The first thing John and Alice need to do, therefore, is to demystify the whole thing. You can make a story out of anything. You can write 100 stories out of a simple object. If Alice's problem is that she simply doesn't know how to begin, John could try a few brain-stretching exercises. Collect 3 or 4 household objects – an apple, a plate, a bell, a box of matches, a pen, a candlestick – whatever comes to hand. Look at each one in turn. See if you and your child can think up a simple story about the first one – 'The Pen': 'A boy buys a pen and takes it to the park where he sits on a bench and writes a letter to his girlfriend. The pen drops out of his pocket and under the bench when he takes the

letter to the post box. The next day the girl brings the
letter to the park to read. She spots the pen under the
bench and uses it to write her reply.' Or simpler still:
'Tom takes a new pen to school. It is borrowed by Oliver
to write his homework and then lent to Ali to copy out his
spellings and passed to Mrs Hobbs to correct the Maths
test and ends up with Rhys who draws a dinosaur before
Tom gets it back at the end of the day and finds it has
quite run out.' Then do the same thing with 'The
Candlestick': 'An old man likes to read by the light of a
candle on a saucer. His daughter worries because the
candle often falls over. One day, in exasperation, she
comes home with a candlestick only to find her father
happily reading by the light of an electric lamp.' Or: 'A
woman on her way home from work spots an unusual
candlestick in the window of the local antique shop. She
takes a fancy to it, buys it, takes it home, unwraps it and
puts it on the kitchen table. She hears her husband
coming in and calling out, 'Look what I found in an
antique shop on the way home!' He comes in and
unwraps an identical candlestick to the one on the table.'

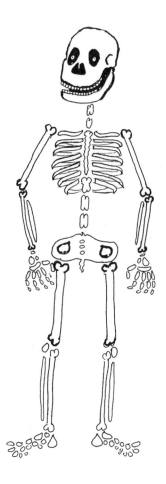

Don't be daunted if these seem beyond you. Between
them, John and Alice will come up with something and
get better at it as they go on. They can do this together
for all the objects, making sure that the stories are clear,
relate to the object throughout and reach an appropriate
ending. Alice should get the idea from this and enjoy
seeing familiar objects in new lights. They may need to
spend several sessions on this.

A related technique – and another good one to help
those for whom planning a consecutive narrative is
problematic – is **skeletons**. John can provide the 'bones'
of a story – four to six crucial points in a narrative. Alice
then has to use her own imagination and creativity to put
on the 'flesh' – fill in the detail. For example:

a) Dad opens the front door. A small dog is there. Dad brings it in. Dog eats meal. Then eats newspaper, carpet, shoes. Dad goes to put dog back outside door. Woman outside asks, 'Have you seen my dog?'

b) Man chops down tree as it blocks light. Next day, garden full of birds squawking angrily at him. Squawking goes on into the night and next day. In desperation, man goes out and buys new tree.

c) New boy in class – no-one takes any notice of him – teacher mentions that his father is a famous footballer/pop star/soap actor – everyone wants to be his friend.

d) Woman on a bus – she finds a lost handbag – searches for the owner – takes it to police station – realises she has left her own bag on the bus.

And so on.

Now might be the time to find your postcard collection (see page 19). John could give Alice a choice of 3 cards, allow her to choose her favourite, get her to plan – in her head but making notes on paper to remind her – a story on the same lines as those they made up together on the objects. Then he should give her 30 minutes to write it down. The same criteria of clarity, relevance and arriving at an end point should apply. Alice should have five minutes for checking (see pages 46–52) and then John should get her to read it aloud to him. After a few of these, Alice should be able to tackle stories from titles such as those given on pages 93–4 with far less hesitation and far more confidence.

Clarity and style

Clarity
Clarity is the essential quality of good writing. This is the most important principle to get across to Alice. It applies

as much to comprehension answers as to essays and, in fact, to any written work in all subjects. Many children have stories quite clear in their own minds but, in the telling of these stories on paper, vital information gets left out. On paper, the story appears to be an unconnected series of moments and ideas. Some children write the story as they would tell it out loud and, on paper, it is muddled, confusing and unpunctuated.

Alice needs to understand that *writing a story is not the same as telling it.* A reader – the person they are writing the story *for* – cannot hear their intonation as they tell the tale, cannot see their facial expressions, cannot understand that, for *them*, 'oh-uh-ar' is their way of expressing their character's gasp of disgust at something she sees. *Alice* might know what she means by this but what help – clues – is she giving her reader? *She* might know that her third sentence is about something that happens the day after what happens in her second sentence but how will the reader if she doesn't explain? Intelligent and imaginative children of this age sometimes find it hard to convey comprehensibly, onto paper, a reality which, in their own minds, is entirely rich and clear.

Writing a story is not the same as telling it.

Ways of working at clarity and style

There are a number of ways this can be got over. Alice needs to understand the *need* for clear explanation. John could start by asking her to describe – out loud – simple objects. He could give her, for example, a spoon, a fork, a lemon, a chair – to look at and then ask her to describe them as if to someone who didn't know what they were or what they looked like. When she has got the idea she can try it in writing. She needs, again, to think of both what the object *looks like* and also what it is *for* or what it *does*. Take, for example, a knife, a cup, a tea-pot, a bottle, a bed, a candle and write a paragraph about each one.

The Blob from Mars

One way of helping Alice with this is to introduce her to **The Blob from Mars**. The Blob is an intelligent creature who can be Alice's pen-friend or, perhaps, someone she chats to by email in cyberspace. The Blob knows and understands a lot about our world and how we live but, now and then, writes back to say that there was a word in Alice's last message he didn't know. Could Alice please explain 'a door' or 'a bucket'? Alice can assume that The Blob understands words such as 'horizontal', 'round' or 'upright' and so on and use them in her explanations.

This approach should help Alice visualise the objects and concentrate on how to convey an idea of them clearly and precisely. It would be a good idea for John to have a go at it himself. It is surprisingly tricky to explain ordinary, everyday objects as though to someone who has no idea of them. Try any of the ones suggested above or others such as a hairbrush, a table, a pencil, a yo-yo, a mug. There is a list on page 90 of further suggestions if this proves a helpful and enjoyable exercise. And you can also think up your own!

Once Alice – and John – have got the idea, they can try more complex – or even abstract – ideas e.g. tiredness, darkness, hunger, a decision, a friend, a fear and so on. However, this should not be tried unless Alice and John feel really comfortable writing about the simpler objects and enjoy a challenge! One way of doing it – as a family game – is to describe an object *without* letting on what it is! Can the family work it out? This will highlight deficiencies in the descriptions.

Stories for younger children

Another approach which may help, if Alice is the sort of girl who leaves out necessary details or who forgets to distinguish between speech and narrative, is to tell her to write a story for a younger child. If she has a younger brother or sister or knows someone else's, the idea of writing something for them will help her concentrate on clear explanation as well as a simple, clearly defined narrative. It might also encourage her not to attempt too complex a plot for her capacities and the available time.

Short sentences

You can't write clearly if you aren't thinking clearly. One way to help the process is – at least in the early stages – to encourage Alice to write very short sentences. To do this, she needs to understand – in the simplest terms – what a sentence is. This book is not intended as an old-fashioned grammar but one or two reminders of the basics may help. You will also find a quick recap. of parts of speech on pages 96–7.

Writing in short sentences can be good practice if stories tend to get out of hand!

Sentences and paragraphs

A sentence can be composed of only two words. 'Sarah ran.' is a perfectly good sentence, made up of a **subject**, i.e. the **person who is doing the action**, in this case, 'Sarah', and 'ran', i.e. what she is **doing** – the **verb**. All sentences need these two components. So, 'the house at the bottom of the road' is not a sentence – it has no verb and 'crying all the way home' is not a sentence as it has no subject. However, 'Sarah ran crying all the way home.' is a fine sentence as is, 'Sarah ran to the house at the bottom of the road.' If Alice gets tangled up in her sentences John could try telling her that a sentence should contain *only one idea*. A sentence should be like a box which has room for one idea. A second idea – even if it is related to the first idea – needs a box of its own. Four or five boxes need to be put together into a suitcase. The suitcase contains all the boxes which have something to do with each other. The suitcase is called a **paragraph**. It may be helpful to look at any simple narrative to see how this works.

Of course, Alice will want to write sentences which have more than two words but this approach may help her to see where sentences could begin and end – among other things, it shows her where full stops are more appropriate than commas, i.e. at the end of a sentence. At the end of a box with one idea in it (see pages 78–89 on punctuation). Although more sophisticated writers will confidently and accurately use longer sentences, at this stage it could well help Alice to box single ideas into individual sentences and to enclose the boxes in a suitcase.

Directions, instruction, description
Another way to help Alice with clarity of both thought and expression, is through practising the writing of directions and instructions. She can practise, for example, writing:

a) **directions** for getting from the kitchen to her bedroom, noting various landmarks such as bookcases, radiators, stairs, doors etc. on the way. This will involve the use of 'right', 'left', 'up', 'down', 'high', 'low' etc. This can be extended to writing about the walk from home to the letter box or to her friend's house or even to school if it's appropriate. The point is that the directions should be clear and accurate enough for a complete stranger – or even a Blob from Mars! – to get from A to B. The skill is in conveying, clearly, a connected account. Missing out turning left at the foot of the stairs will have the reader walking into a wall!

Simple actions and straightforward journeys may not be easy to describe.

b) **instructions** – putting a duvet into a duvet cover, making a sandwich, watering plants. Simple actions are actually not at all simple to describe. The Blob from Mars can be a good friend again here. He needs to be told exactly – step-by-step – how one polishes shoes, cleans out a guinea pig's cage, fills a fountain pen, makes a plait etc. John will need to have a go at writing a few of these to see what is involved. The important thing in each case is, again, accurate detail. If the sandwich description doesn't make clear that the buttered sides are made to face each other, the Blob would have very greasy fingers – if Blobs have fingers!

c) **description**. Alice should understand from this the importance of *detail*. Children – and their parents – get very hung up on the idea of *description* in stories because they are constantly told of the need for it by their teachers. They need to understand why it is important. It is important in stories for the same reasons as it is important in instructions or directions. Suppose Alice is set the title, 'The Picnic'. Here are two very different approaches:

i) Karim and Naveen went for a picnic. They went to the park and met James and Richard there. They decided to play cricket before eating the picnic. The park was full of people. Then a dog came and ran off with their ball. They chased the dog all over the park and round the pond. Then the dog jumped into the pond and dropped the ball. He then came out and shook himself all over the boys. Naveen got very cross but Karim laughed and dropped the picnic. The dog jumped on the sandwiches and ate them.

Or:

ii) It was a lovely day so Karim and Naveen decided to go for a picnic. They spent ages making all their favourite sandwiches – peanut butter with marmite, pickle and egg and strawberry jam. Karim had to stop Naveen eating most of them as he wrapped them up! They gathered their cricket bats and a ball and strolled down to the park where they bumped into James and Richard. They agreed to play cricket first and have the picnic afterwards. Suddenly, James hit a ball into the

41

bushes and a large black and white dog raced in after it. He charged off to the other side of the park with all the boys galloping after him, yelling and waving their bats. The dog was having a lovely time and ended up by jumping into the pond, dropping the ball and laughing at them. He then came out and shook himself energetically, drenching the boys. Naveen was furious but Karim laughed so much that he dropped the picnic. The dog was delighted, jumped on the sandwiches and gobbled them up.

The point is clear. Alice and John could look at the above examples and see what a difference the detail makes. The stories are, of course, identical but the scenes are far more vivid in the second example and help the reader to imagine and enjoy the story.

Alice could consider what kinds of detail help in a story – the weather, the place and surroundings, the mood and atmosphere, the characters and their appearance and so on.

Vocabulary

You will have noticed that the second of the above extracts differed from the first in some of the words used. For example, where i had 'went', ii had 'strolled' and where i had 'ran', ii had 'charged' and so on. Also, there were other examples of more interesting vocabulary in ii: 'galloping', 'energetically', 'drenched', 'furious' etc., words with which Alice should be familiar – even if she wouldn't naturally use them herself. They make a piece of writing more varied and, as we said above, Alice should be encouraged to try out such words **from her own vocabulary**.

As we have said, learning words in a vacuum is of limited value. However, when a new word is encountered, Alice should be encouraged to use it – correctly – in her writing and speaking. Parents can help with this by using the word themselves and pointing out its use – in as unforced a manner as possible! The **spelling book**, mentioned above on page 19, is of additional use here, functioning, as it does, as a child's personal dictionary. Nevertheless, it is important to remember that the accurate use of simple words is of more value than the inaccurate or unconfident use of grander ones.

Dictionaries

Although there is no merit in the use of long and complex words for their own sake, and although parents should be suspicious of teachers who set lists of such words for learning, children should acquire an increasingly sophisticated vocabulary through their own reading and from being encouraged to look up in a *dictionary* words they do not know – or to ask adults. A good dictionary should always be on hand and it should be normal for Alice and Rajiv to see John and Jyoti looking up words for their own information. Dictionaries are sources – not only of knowledge – but of fun. You can play any number of word games with a dictionary. It may, for example, be fun for Alice and Rajiv to open the dictionary, find a word and see if John or Jyoti can tell them what it means! or they can read the definition of a familiar word and see if their parents can work out what it is defining. For example, 'A space within a building enclosed by its own walls, ceiling and floor', is a definition given in Webster's dictionary of – a 'room'. John and Jyoti might find that quite a challenge! It is, in any case, fun – and useful – to just look at how a dictionary entry is constructed with part of speech, pronunciation, derivation and so on – whether or not John and Jyoti feel competent to explain the various hieroglyphics! Certainly, Alice and Rajiv should feel comfortable and familiar with the use of a dictionary and should, ideally, by this stage, have an approachable-looking one of their own.

Dictionaries are not only tools but also the source of a lot of fun.

More on vocabulary

Again in the interests of clarity, accuracy and the involvement of the reader, Alice needs to become increasingly confident in her use of words. This should be an enjoyable process. Look at the two passages below and see how much more lively they would be if the words used were substituted for those in brackets:

a) 'You're not going to watch that gardening programme?' said (gasped) Karim.
   'Yes, I am,' said (replied) Mum.
   'But I've got to watch the football on the other side,' said (exclaimed) Karim.
   'I'm afraid not,' said (disagreed) Mum. 'You know I always watch this programme.'
   'But it's the final,' said (protested) Karim. 'I've waited all season for this and one gardening programme is just like any other.'
   'Not to me it isn't,' said (smiled) Mum. 'You'll have to go round to Naveen's.'

b) Sarah went (crept) out of the classroom. She went (slunk) out of school, sucking her lolly. She went (dawdled) along the road and went (slouched) past the shops, the cinema and her brother's nursery. As she went (trudged) down her own street, she went (plodded) even more slowly. How could she give her mother the letter from her teacher?

The point makes itself. Helping Alice and Rajiv realise the potential they have for livening up their writing in this way should be fun and can involve the whole family. You need to meet George and Helen.

'It's raining,' George _____ .
The blank after 'George' can be filled with anything other

than the colourless 'said'.

You can find words which convey:

a) pleasure, e.g. cheered, laughed, hooted – perhaps
   George is a farmer with crops dying for lack of rain

b) sadness, e.g. sighed, sniffed, wept – perhaps George
   has planned an outdoor birthday party

c) boredom or tiredness, e.g. yawned, muttered, grizzled –
   perhaps George has waited all day to go out

d) disbelief, e.g. gasped, repeated, queried – perhaps
   George is in the Sahara Desert!

e) fury e.g. bellowed, roared, fumed – perhaps George has
   just finished painting the shed

There are any number of other circumstances and words to go with them. This is a good family activity. Upwards of 200 substitutes for 'said' can be found by imaginative collaboration just using ordinary words. A good tip is to remember the number of words we use for speaking which originate from our expression of animal noises e.g. 'It's raining,' George 'whined', 'growled', 'hissed', 'chirped', 'purred', 'bellowed', 'cackled', 'barked' etc.

Helen _____ up the road.

The blank after 'Helen' can be filled with any single verb which could replace 'went' plus an adverb. For example, instead of 'went slowly' we would use 'dawdled' or 'ambled'. Instead of 'went quickly' we would use 'raced' or 'charged'. The point is to avoid the featureless 'went' – as we did above with 'said' and to choose a word with more colour, adding life and flavour to the writing. Again, you should think in terms of Helen's mood, her age and size, the time of day, the weather and so on. Again, remember how we used verbs we associate with *animals*.

'George' and 'Helen' can be fun for the whole family.

Here are a few suggestions: Helen stumbled/ tottered/ skipped/ bounced/ galloped/ limped/ charged/ skidded/ waded/ limped/ crawled/ slithered/ stalked.

You could aim for over 150 if the whole family collaborates. There are lists of possible substitutes for 'said' and for 'went' on pages 119–120 but don't look till you've had a good try! Alice and Rajiv will be delighted with their collection and will want to incorporate such verbs, aptly and imaginatively, in their narratives. Alternatives to 'said' are especially useful when you come to tackle the writing of **conversation** (see pages 81–3).

Adjectives and adverbs

Adjectives are describing words which tell you more about nouns (nouns, if you remember, are the names of persons, places, things, e.g. Rajiv, Manchester, table). Adjectives are words like these: 'a *wrinkled* face', 'a *grumpy* boss', 'a *breezy* day', 'a *torn* shirt', 'an *old* town', 'a *tired* smile', 'a *hard* decision' and 'a *loveable* teacher'.

Adverbs tell you more about verbs (verbs, you will recall, are doing words, e.g. think, speak, eat, worked, laughed, will go, shall meet, did hope, have thought etc.)

Adverbs tell you more about the **how**, **when** or **where** of the verbs, e.g. 'he shouted *harshly*', 'they sang *loudly*', 'she wrote *lengthily*', 'they walked *away*' and 'he worked *late*'. They, again, add more detail to an account – helping to convey the quality, mood, atmosphere of an experience and Alice and Rajiv need to understand their usefulness in doing this. There are more examples on pages 96–7 and Rajiv and Alice may want to make their own collection as a way of reminding themselves of their importance.

Checking

Why on earth devote a whole separate section to checking? Surely, just a careful read-through is enough? Think about it. How often have you read through something you've written, passed it as perfect and been horrified to see it a day or so later – or, worse still, be given it back by someone else – full of mistakes that you never noticed and you feel sure someone else must have put them in after you finished?

The normal thing is to read what one *thinks* is there. This is even more true if one checks minutes after putting down one's pen. Checking, therefore, is better put off as long as possible – a bit like going back to a crossword you are stuck on after an hour or two and suddenly seeing, quite plainly, all the answers that stumped you before.

Computers

A reminder that Rajiv and Alice should be barred from the computer for this type of work. They need to develop a spell check inside their own heads – they won't have a computer in the exams!

Acquiring checking methods and habits is of great value – firstly because it develops confidence and gradually incorporates the essential skills into one's writing and secondly because, in an exam, it can save vital marks. Here are a number of methods which you can try, on both comprehension answers and on essays.

There are many ways of checking. See which works best for you.

Comprehensions

If at all possible, time needs to be left at the end of comprehension tests for checking. Checking can reveal all kinds of errors – factual, lexical and grammatical – which Rajiv will have missed when writing his answers and can, therefore, recoup vital marks. Ideally, Rajiv will have time to read through his answers carefully *twice*.

The aim of the **first read-through** should be to discover whether his answers:

a) actually answer the question he was asked

47

b) answer *all* the question he was asked

c) explain clearly and accurately what he wants to say.

The **second read-through** is to find spelling and punctuation errors or omissions. If Rajiv knows that he has a tendency to make mistakes with, for example, double letters, e.g. he writes 'stoping' for 'stopping', he can be particularly on the look-out for these. He may need to be reminded about the punctuation of sentences, i.e. the use of full stops rather than repeated commas. Examiners, understandably, take an especially dim view of words incorrectly copied from the paper!

Essays

Similarly an essay should be checked *twice* – **firstly** to ensure that the story it tells will be clear to a reader; that essential information is given, not assumed; that speech is attributed – correctly; that the essay makes sense. **Secondly**, as for comprehensions, spelling and punctuation need to be checked, with particular attention to habitual mistakes and the punctuation of conversation.

Developing the habit of checking

Rajiv and Alice may well put down their pens at the end of an exercise with a smile and say 'finished'. If to the question, 'have you checked it?' they answer 'no', then Jyoti's and John's response is, 'then you *haven't* finished.' Preparation for the exams needs to include checking – in different forms – as an *integral* part of the exercise. It is equally important for any other written work to be handed in. Some of the methods of checking given below cannot be carried out in an exam context but most can. What matters is that Rajiv and Alice understand the importance of it. Systematic checking and the improvements they will make during the process will soon prove to them how important it is.

Checking methods

Check method 1

This is only possible out of the exam context. It is helpful for both essays and comprehensions. It is simply to **read aloud**, *word by word*, what has been written. The word-by-word bit is important. Many children – and adults – read what they *think* is there. If each word is carefully pronounced, anything missing or anything nonsensical should be obvious. Either way, developing the habit of reading for meaning in this way is invaluable and acquiring this awareness and technique will help during *silent* checking in exams.

Check method 2

The reading aloud of both essays and comprehension answers should, primarily, be to make sure that what is written says what Rajiv and Alice *meant* to say. Reading – aloud or silently – is also important for answering the following questions: 'Is what is written *clear*? sufficiently *detailed*? sufficiently *explanatory*? Is it *repetitious*? Are there *errors*? Are there failures of *consistency*?' (e.g. at the start of the story Ben is taller than Luke but shorter by the end). This check is for **meaning** and **clarity**.

Mistakes have a life of their own and crawl in when no-one's looking!

Check method 3 and The Magic Nasty Teacher

This is for accuracy in **spelling**, **sentence**- and **paragraph**-making and **punctuation**. Alice and Rajiv should know the rules by this time but have they stuck to them? It is remarkably difficult to spot your own mistakes but horribly obvious when they are pointed out by someone else. This is where adults – of two kinds!- can help. Supposing Alice has written a good piece but John can see a number of mistakes of the kind mentioned above which Alice has not spotted. It is best if Alice finds these for herself. John can help by putting a dot in the

margin of every line in which there is a punctuation error or an omission and a 'sp' for every spelling. He can then tell Alice to check again and she will, this time, pick up quite a few more. However, if she just can't see them and all else fails, John will need to invoke the assistance of a terrible and terrifying individual known as **The Magic Nasty Teacher!**

Parents will know whether or not this is likely to work for their child. It depends on a willingness to join with the parent in making up an imaginary teacher who is simply the meanest and most horrible in the world. She loves mistakes! She can smell them out! Spot them anywhere! She loves them because she can underline them in bright red ink and make whoever has committed them feel very, very small. She will cackle with joy at the sight of a missed 'e' before '-ly', e.g. in 'sincer(e)ly', at single letters which ought to be double, e.g. 'sliped' for 'slipped' and just pounces on habitual mistakes like 'intrested' (for 'interested'), 'definate' (for 'definite') and 'propaly' (for 'properly') and so on. She sees mistakes which weren't even there before she came along! The test works like this. John will, for example, wave a wand (pencil?), clap his hands, say a magic word and – hey presto! – Alice is transformed into this very Magic Nasty Teacher and is instantly, fiercely on the warpath for mistakes. If Alice can enter into the spirit of this, she will suddenly spot mistakes which, before, she just did not see and go at them with gusto! Punctuation should be put in and spelling mistakes should be underlined – in red if Alice really wants to be fierce – and then, on a separate sheet, the words should be practised until a version is found which looks better. There are any number of variations on The Magic Nasty Teacher Test. These will depend on the Parent–Child dynamic. Some children will not feel comfortable with it. With the right child it can transform their approach to checking and amaze them!

Check method 4

This is **The Visualisation Test**. Some children who have a good visual imagination may find this method more helpful for correcting spelling errors than The Magic Nasty Teacher. The trick is to identify a word which doesn't look correctly spelled and to try and picture it as it would look in a newspaper headline or on a large advertising hoarding. For example, if Alice has written 'suprise' for 'surprise' and she knows it looks wrong but can't work out why, John could suggest that she shut her eyes and try to picture a newspaper headline saying something like, 'Teachers Call Surprise Strike', or an advertisement saying, 'Surprise Your Taste Buds'. Miraculously, after a moment's concentration, some children, given this technique, can suddenly see the entire word, correctly spelled, i.e. it is there, in their memories and it just needs real concentration to picture it accurately in their mind's eye. If this doesn't work for Alice, John shouldn't push it. Many children – and adults – go completely blank if asked to 'picture' anything!

Check method 5

This is the use of **Rhyme**. This is far from being fool-proof, English spelling being so diverse and inconsistent. However, if Alice is stuck for the spelling of a word, it *can* help to think up a rhyme for the word she is trying to spell. For example, if she isn't sure of how to spell 'gravel' she may be able to arrive at it via 'travel'. The less helpful side of this is that trying to find a rhyme for, for example, 'straight', could produce 'late', 'trait', 'freight' and so on! No-one ever said that English spelling is straightforward!

Rhyme *can* help but don't rely on it!

Check method 6

All children will be familiar with the technique of writing and rewriting a word until it looks correct. However, this is an invaluable method, one which requires patience and perseverance but which, with most children, has its own rewards. It should be encouraged and practised. Many children are tempted to give up. 'I don't know' – comes too quickly. Trying to get it right until you do, should be encouraged and warm praise given if it works.

Punctuation and spelling

Punctuation

The main problems at this stage are usually in making distinctions between commas and full stops, the correct use of apostrophes and the punctuation of conversation. Alice and Rajiv need to be clear about commas, full stops, question marks, exclamation marks, speech marks, when to start a new line, when to indent, (i.e. to start a new line further along the line than usual) and apostrophes. The fear of apostrophes alone can practically traumatise a child. However, they are simple if two basic rules are followed and these are covered below on page 83–6. If John is not quite sure he is comfortable with the use of apostrophes it would be well for him to familiarise himself with their use before he initiates Alice! Punctuation is dealt with in detail on pages 78–89.

Spelling

It is easy for parents who naturally spell correctly and who cannot remember a time when they didn't, to get particularly wound-up about inaccurate or inconsistent spelling. It is also true that, despite recent changes in the prioritising of literacy in schools, there is less emphasis on the importance of spelling accuracy than there was when most of today's grandparents were at school.

Many of today's parents acquired their good spelling in the decades since leaving school. John and Jyoti will need an especially strong grip on their patience if they are to work on spelling! Alice and Rajiv's inconsistency and sudden memory loss when it comes to spelling even quite ordinary words may seem quite baffling. Alice may be able to spell 'finally' correctly on one line of her essay and *always* manages it in tests but will write it as 'finaly' elsewhere when she is concentrating on other things. It is at this point that John will need to remind himself that Alice *wants* to get it right – she is not doing it to infuriate him! What can be done?

Learning lists of words has *some*, but limited, value. This is also true of copying out a word a dozen times or more – the staple, old-fashioned remedy. Alice and Rajiv will have been taught methods of learning spellings at school – ways such as studying, covering, copying and so on. Learning words in practice, as you meet them, is the best way. Nonetheless, you will find on pages 62–3 a list of commonly misspelled words and John and Jyoti will do well, gradually and in as natural a way as possible, to check that Alice and Rajiv are confident about them.

Spelling Book

When Jyoti begins working with Rajiv, she should buy him an exercise book (see page 19) At the same time, it is a good idea to buy what will become his **spelling book**. The ideal thing for this is a large **address book** – a no frills, spiral-bound, indexed notebook, still to be found in stationers. It should have an alphabetical index, plain lined pages but preferably no special spaces for telephone numbers, email addresses and so on. It should have at least one page for each letter.

The idea is that whenever Rajiv misspells a word or if he meets a new word and wants to learn it, or if he is given words to learn, these words go immediately into his own spelling book. He will, thereby, build up his own unique and personal dictionary of necessary words.

Your spelling book is your most useful tool.

Ideally, each time he needs to write in a new word, he will spend a minute looking over the words already on this page. So, for example, if he misspells 'sausage' he will find his 's' page and remind himself of 'surprise', 'success', 'special' and 'several' or whatever else happens to be there. Every now and then, he should be given the task of learning the accumulated words and then be tested – perhaps ten words at a time. He will enjoy the sense of achievement this gives him. Also, as all these words should have arisen out of his own work, they are words he knows and knows he wants. He will, therefore, understand the point of knowing how to spell them. Giving him lists of complex words he doesn't use is of very little value – and makes little sense to him.

More spelling techniques

It is extraordinary how often a child will miscopy a word. A tip is to copy a word in groups of letters, say, three letters at a time. If, for example, Alice is copying out 'necessary', she could study the first 3 letters – 'nec' and hold them in her head while she covers the word and copies them out, then do the same with 'ess' and finish with 'ary'. This way she has to really concentrate as she does it and this will be an aid to memorising the word. She should be familiar with such techniques from school.

Make a picture by writing the word over and over again in such a way that it makes a design. For example a word picture of 'ball' could be made out of the word 'ball' written many times over.

Another idea – more fun than merely copying out words in a list – is to make a **Word Picture**. This can be an abstract pattern for words such as 'necessary', something more imaginative and illustrative for words such as 'surprise' and something literal for words such as 'bicycle'. Alice and Rajiv – unless they really hate drawing! – will enjoy this and it is another way of helping words stick.

This book does not purport to be a spelling manual. It would be book-length on spelling alone if it were! However, in addition to the list of words on pages 62–3, you will also find examples of common mistakes and ways of eradicating them on pages 63–78 along with some helpful rules, games and guidelines.

Dyslexia

Few children are dyslexic but those who are, especially if the dyslexia is severe, do need help and as early in their school careers as possible. First of all, though, they need the problem to be recognised and acknowledged. A child with a known dyslexia problem is entitled to special consideration, specialised support in school and also to have more time in exams. If you suspect that your child may be dyslexic, the *worst* thing you can do is to hope no-one will notice. All good selective schools – as well as non-selective ones – now have well-established support teaching for students with dyslexia and other learning difficulties. They also thoroughly understand that these have no bearing whatever on actual intelligence or ability.

Dyslexia only becomes a serious problem if it is not identified and if no help is given.

Dyslexia should have been picked up at school by your child's teachers well before this stage. However, especially if she or he is diligent and conscientious, it frequently isn't. This is for two reasons. Firstly, the teacher's limited time and energies are often taken up in dealing with children who are less able and more demanding than Alice. Children like her can miss out on this vital attention. Secondly, able but dyslexic children can be extraordinarily skilful in evolving strategies to compensate for their difficulties. It can sometimes take an experienced and sharp-eyed teacher to spot these adroit evasions and manoeuvrings.

Here is a brief list of things to look out for. If Alice does more than one or two of these on a regular basis then it may be as well to consider having her assessed for dyslexia:

55

a) confusion of letters, e.g. 'b' for 'd' or 'u' for 'n"

b) confusion of letters which sound similar, e.g. 'th' for 'v" or 'f'

c) reversing letters or words e.g. 'pot' for 'top' or 'stop' for 'post'

d) leaving words out

e) repeating words

f) confusing short words, e.g. 'of' instead of 'for'

g) slowness and difficulty with reading, e.g. losing one's place, slipping onto the line below, mispronouncing familiar words, lack of expression

h) difficulty writing on the line

i) problems in making letters

j) shortening words, e.g. 'rember' for 'remember'

k) getting tired very quickly when writing

l) gripping the pencil too tightly or pressing very hard with it

m) slow to learn right and left

n) slow to learn maths tables and sequences like days of the week, months etc.

Dyslexia can be mild, moderate or severe. Help is available and it is important that you seek it promptly. Alice's teacher or Head Teacher is the right place to get support or, if necessary, you can contact the **Local Education Authority's Extra Learning Support Department**. There will also be a branch of **Parent Partnership** which will help John find the best help for Alice. Finally, there is the excellent **British Dyslexia Association** which will understand your concerns and will have all kinds of suggestions as to what to do next and how to go about it.

It is worth repeating that a 'label' of dyslexia, dyspraxia or whatever, is not a stigma but an invaluable tool for unlocking support and understanding. Sorting out dyslexia is the most positive and educationally vital thing a parent can do for an affected child. Alice will be hugely relieved and eternally grateful to have her problem identified, understood and assisted. However, it is still sadly true that local authorities – and schools – vary greatly in the provision they make for supporting children with special educational needs of the dyslexia variety. If you are concerned, you will need to do some research on the attitudes of local Heads and on the support your child will receive in schools you are considering. It shouldn't be necessary but, in some cases, it still is. Finally, up-to-date research suggests that, far from being educationally disabling, dyslexia may even bring with it actual benefits. Dyslexics seem to have particular abilities, especially in areas of creativity and problem-solving. The British Dyslexia Association will be able to tell you of many high-profile dyslexics who are positively grateful for the condition and who attribute their success to the way their own particular minds work – dyslexia and all. If your child is affected, his or her self-esteem will benefit from knowing this kind of thing and this knowledge cannot come too soon!

Starting post

If you have got this far, you have done very well and are quite ready to begin. You understand what you are hoping to achieve and have methods at your fingertips. The previous pages have already given you a number of exercises, methods and techniques to help your child with the basics. Part Two provides more exercises to help develop these basics and to explain some common problems and ways of combating them. The final part will give you and your child some practice in the sorts of exercises they will meet at 11+. A final word of caution.

A relaxed and collaborative approach is essential for progress. If you are fighting - stop!

Nothing is more important than family relationships and harmony. Some parents and children can work in good-humoured and constructive collaboration. It is fun and the emphasis is on 'giving it a go.' This approach stands a good chance of making some real difference to the child's performance in English and his or her confidence as a result. If the attempt to work on some of the methods described here result in confrontation and misery then STOP! It won't be constructive but harmful – both to family relationships and to your child's confidence. It won't help his or her performance either. Having taken this in, along with the advice on the previous pages, with a song in your heart and without any feeling of make or break, you are ready to turn the page!

PART TWO

Introduction

This part is designed to help parents deal with some of the problems that children aged 10–12 have with their written work. However, the examples and exercises in Parts Two and Three are of little value on their own and using this book merely to put Alice or Rajiv though the exercises without their parents having read and taken in all that is in the preceding pages will achieve little. Jyoti and John will, ideally, discuss the examples on the following pages with Rajiv and Alice, explaining to them the purpose and the technique in each case. The book can't, of course, cover every possible difficulty but there is remarkable uniformity at this stage with respect to common problems and these are covered here. The chances are that your child will make some or all of these errors in their work! Jyoti and John recognise them all! – but Alice has more problems with basic accuracy than Rajiv.

Spellings and Related Problems

Spelling List

The best source of words to practise is Alice's own spelling book (see pages 53–4) and the list below, taken from such a book, may serve as a reminder to other children of words they *understand* and want to remember how to *spell*. Ideally, all the words here should be part of an 11-year-old's vocabulary – both to use confidently in their own writing and to spell correctly when required. However, drilling a child to learn this – or any other – set of words is not a good use of precious time and is more likely to increase stress and distress than to achieve anything worthwhile. The list is here as a guide to the range and level of

vocabulary that Alice should be aiming for in her own book and memory. Many of these words are seen as tricky by the average child and their acquisition may be a laborious process. To absorb them naturally in the course of other work is best and routine learning practice can be part of that – in small doses! The best thing is for Alice to read them and then to use them as seems natural in her own writing. This is, of course, a highly selective list and Rajiv's list may well look very different.

absolutely	definitely	immediately
accident	delicious	important
actually	desperate	interested
another	different	interesting
answered	disappeared	January
article	disappoint	jealous
August	discussed	juice
author	edge	laughter
a lot (as two words)	eight	library
beautiful	embarrassed	listened
beginning	especially	lose
believe	excited	machine
biscuit	extremely	majesty
ceiling	favourite	measure
certain	February	minute
chief	figure	mountain
choose	finally	natural
colour	friend	necessary
completely	gadget	no-one
concentration	giant	normally
concrete	guard	nuisance
dangerous	guide	occasion
deceive	guitar	opportunity
decided	horrible	orchestra
decision	hour	parallel
	imagine	parents

peculiar	separate	through
people	several	tomorrow
piece	sincerely	tongue
position	straight	tragedy
prejudice	strength	tunnel
probably	successful	until
properly	sure	unusual
receive	surprise	usually
recognise	suspicious	Wednesday
remember	system	weight
sausage	terrified	which
scared	thought	wizard

Common spelling confusions

Adding '-ly'

These two innocent letters cause endless, unnecessary confusion. '-ly' is usually added to an adjective, e.g. 'happy', to make an adverb, e.g. 'happily'. Confusion arises in several areas but can be quickly dispelled.

a) *Adding '-ly' to words which end in '-y', e.g. 'happy'* → *'happily'*:

The 'y' changes to an 'i'. Practise with 'pretty', 'sunny', 'dozy', 'crazy', 'funny', 'cosy', 'gloomy', 'wavy', 'shiny' etc.

b) *Adding '-ly' to words which end in '-l', e.g. 'final', 'wonderful', 'normal'*:

These words do not shed their existing 'l'. In other words they have 2 'l's and become 'finally', 'wonderfully' and 'normally'. Practise with these and 'actual', 'formal', 'hopeful', 'casual', 'practical', 'helpful', 'total', 'special', 'careful', 'natural', 'partial', 'hysterical', 'topical', 'typical', 'usual', 'merciful' etc. It's worth learning, as a matter of course, that words ending in '-ful' always have a double 'l' when they change to being '-fully' words. So, in addition to those above, you have 'thoughtfully', 'cheerfully', 'doubtfully',

Adding 'ly' need not cause sleepless nights!

'thankfully', 'rightfully' and so on.

c) *Adding '-ly' to words which end in '-e', e.g. 'extreme' or 'wise':*

These words do not – in general – drop the final 'e'. They become 'extremely' and 'wisely'. Practise with these and 'aggressive', 'close', 'brave', 'remote', 'safe', 'polite', 'late' etc.

Exceptions are when there is more than one consonant before the 'e', e.g. 'amiable' → 'amiably', 'humble' → 'humbly', 'simple' → 'simply', etc. A second exception is words ending in '-ue', e.g. 'due' → 'duly', 'true' → 'truly'. These can be learned separately.

d) *Finally:*

It is *always* '-ly', *never* '-ley' – as many children like to think.

Adding '-ed'

This basic and obvious suffix causes an extraordinary amount of difficulty with some children. The confusion is sometimes caused because, in some words, e.g. 'hated' or 'sorted', the '-ed' is actually *pronounced*. This is always the case with words that end in '-ted'. However, most past tense words which end in '-ed' do not pronounce the suffix but the spelling is still the same. If Alice writes 'slippd' for 'slipped' or 'tamd' for 'tamed' then she will need to learn and practise the '-ed' ending.

John could point out that some words already end in an 'e' and she will need only to add the 'd', e.g. 'cope' becomes 'coped', 'swipe' becomes 'swiped' and so on. However, it is more helpful to think of all regular verbs as ending in '-ed' in the past tense – whether or not they have an 'e' ending in the present! John could get Alice to turn the following words into their past tense equivalents, e.g. 'wash' → 'washed':

battle	grope	rake
clatter	hope	smile
climb	joke	sniff
cuddle	like	surprise
flatter	limp	tame
fritter	live	thrill
grate	poke	tramp
groan	praise	walk

It may be more fun for John to construct sentences which Alice can put into the past tense in their entirety. For example:

Sarah and Laura (pour) the popcorn into a bowl and (start) to munch.

Or:

Karim and Naveen (walk) to the park and (bump) into some friends.

Double letters

Adding '-ed' or '-ing' to a word can mean doubling the final letter of that word, e.g. 'stop' becomes 'stopped'/'stopping' and 'chat' becomes 'chatted'/'chatting'.

Words which do this almost all end in 'b', 'g', 'l', 'm', 'n', 'p' or 't'.

Here are some common examples, using the '-ed' suffix:

bat →	batted		hum →	hummed
bin →	binned		instil →	instilled
bob →	bobbed		jut →	jutted
chug →	chugged		knit →	knitted
dim →	dimmed		lag →	lagged
drip →	dripped		ram →	rammed
fan →	fanned		rap →	rapped
fulfil →	fulfilled		rebel →	rebelled
hop →	hopped		rig →	rigged

65

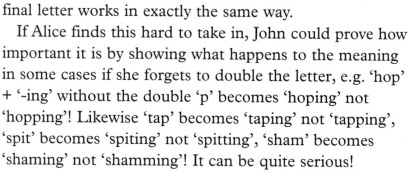

rub →   rubbed   stab →   stabbed

shop →   shopped   stun →   stunned

Not doubling a letter where necessary can cause some strange changes in meaning!

Adding '-ing' to any of the above words by doubling the final letter works in exactly the same way.

If Alice finds this hard to take in, John could prove how important it is by showing what happens to the meaning in some cases if she forgets to double the letter, e.g. 'hop' + '-ing' without the double 'p' becomes 'hoping' not 'hopping'! Likewise 'tap' becomes 'taping' not 'tapping', 'spit' becomes 'spiting' not 'spitting', 'sham' becomes 'shaming' not 'shamming'! It can be quite serious!

John could ask Alice to add '-ing' or '-ed' to the following words remembering to double the final letter:

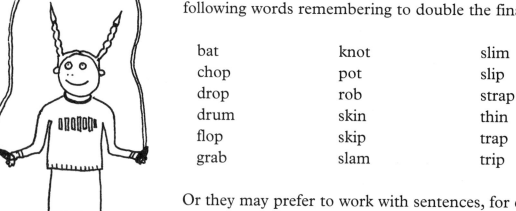

bat	knot	slim
chop	pot	slip
drop	rob	strap
drum	skin	thin
flop	skip	trap
grab	slam	trip

Or they may prefer to work with sentences, for example:
Sarah and Laura (chop) firewood for the bonfire and (drop) a lighted match to start it off.
Or:
Karim and Naveen (trap) the thief who (mug) their friend last week.

John may like to bear in mind, in case it helps, that you never have double letters after double vowels, e.g. 'ai', 'ea', 'oa', 'oo', 'oi', 'ui' or after long single vowels e.g. 'a' pronounced 'ay', 'e' pronounced 'ee', 'i' pronounced 'eye', 'o' pronounced 'oh' or 'u' pronounced 'you'.

Words ending in '-ous' or '-ious'

Lots of words end with these groups of letters and, when '-ious' is preceded by a 'c', or a 't' – making a 'sh' sound as in 'cautious' or 'suspicious', they can cause some anxiety and need time spent on them. There is little John and Jyoti can do other than help Alice and Rajiv recognise and become familiar with these words and simply practise their use. Here is a selective list of such words that Alice and Rajiv may come across most frequently:

-ous	**-ious**
ambidextrous	ambitious
anonymous	amphibious
arduous	anxious
barbarous	cautious
bulbous	curious
disastrous	delicious
fabulous	laborious
glamorous	malicious
gluttonous	precious
horrendous	religious
nervous	superstitious
raucous	suspicious
scandalous	vicious

There are also, of course, those words which end in '-eous', e.g. 'gorgeous', 'hideous', 'righteous' but John and Jyoti might well wait till Alice and Rajiv are ready for these! The 'sh' sound found in many of the '-ious' words above is also found in words which end in '-tion' or '-ssion', e.g. 'caution', 'action', 'passion', 'session' and so on. It may be helpful for Alice and Rajiv to make a list of as many of these words as they can think of.

Words ending in '-ough'

The oddest and trickiest group of words in all English

spelling and the source of endless nightmares for learners of English as a foreign language. Fortunately, most native speakers acquire familiarity with the various pronunciations of this group of letters just as a matter of course. However, they are a source of anxiety for anxious spellers who start to put in '-ough's all over the place. It's as well to learn these most common examples and to point out that, in general use, Rajiv and Alice are unlikely to need any others. It's also a good idea to point out to them how cleverly they can read such words – knowing automatically to pronounce them correctly, despite the seven different ways in which this group of four letters can be pronounced!

Imagine what these are like for learners of English from abroad!

1. cough	3. though	6. Slough
trough	although	7. brought
2. enough	4. through	bought
tough	5. thorough	ought
rough	borough	thought

Unscrambling and other games

There are any number of word games that will help develop spelling techniques and confidence. Just about any word game will have some benefit as they all help children feel more comfortable and familiar with words and make the formation of words seem less worrying and more fun. **Scrabble**, the junior version to start with, and the various games based on **anagrams** – the making of a word from the letters of another word, e.g. 'bleat' from the letters in 'table' – are all worthwhile. There is also the classic parlour game of taking a word and forming other words from different groups of its letters. This is a good one for building confidence as you can start small and make bigger and bigger words. Take, for example, the word 'playground'. Alice could start by finding three-letter words, e.g. 'pal', 'lay', 'pay', 'dog', 'lap' and so on.

She could graduate to four-letter words e.g. 'gulp', 'pray', 'drop', 'load' and so on and may soon be able to see even five or six letter words aplenty! Newsagents stock lots of puzzle magazines and John and Alice could have fun working through Wordsearches, simple crosswords and so on as well as playing more formal boxed games or making up their own.

Usually, the favourite game at this stage is **Unscrambling** and this, like other games, can be tailored to suit the interests of an individual child. A child who is very unconfident about spelling can make great progress when an involving game is introduced and the spelling work develops an interest of its own. The idea is to muddle up the letters of a word and for the child to unscramble the muddle to discover the word. Jyoti tried it with Rajiv whose spelling was, for a while, a problem but whose passion for Leeds United Football Club was not! So Jyoti muddled up the names of various football clubs listed below. See how many you can unscramble!

All word games make for good practice and are enjoyable for the whole family.

pruss	plovrileo	snato lival
seled	stew mah	noblot
cleesha	lensara	rynuble
mafluh	lubbknarc	westclane

She also scrambled the names of some of his favourite players, foods, friends, local shops, familiar animals, towns, countries, colours, means of transport and so on. Here are some examples you could try – but also make up your own! (Answers on page 115 if you get stuck.) When Rajiv gets the idea, he will enjoy – carefully! – scrambling up other words for Jyoti and the rest of the family. Mistakes are unforgivable in this game – for obvious reasons!

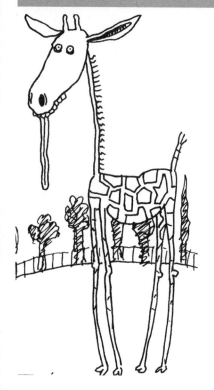

Animals	Colours	English Towns	Foods
fabfoul	wolley	slibrot	zazip
yemnok	lebu	thrignob	agussea
grite	gorean	noodln	nacob
noli	voteli	desel	pisch
frigfea	lescrat	roky	asdal
plateenh	wornb	mudhar	esheec
droolicce	vyna	tocyvern	aspat
bartib	nereg	drove	rycru
phese	ewith	nicnoll	chindaws
flow	yerg	rowchin	realce

Common confusions and mistakes

They're/there/their
These are commonly confused as they sound the same. It is helpful to remind oneself of their *correct* usages:

a) Laura and Sarah will be late. *They're* (i.e. *they are*) staying at school for a rehearsal. *They're* my best friends.
b) *There* (i.e. in a particular place – though this is only one use of this word) is my house. The one over *there*. *There* is no-one in. I don't think *there* is any food either! (*There is* needs to be learned as a very common phrase.)
c) I've put *their* (i.e. belonging to them) dinner in the fridge. They've gone to *their* friend's house. They like to do *their* homework together.

Here is an exercise. Fill in the gaps with the appropriate word. John could make up more such exercises for Alice or she could write her own sentences using these words correctly.

Where are the boys? T_____ looking for _____ football.
It went somewhere over _____, in the bushes. T_____

probably crawling about on _____ hands and knees getting _____ trousers muddy. It's nearly dark now so _____ isn't much point carrying on looking. T_____ probably just enjoying getting dirty!

Wear/where/were/we're
This is a collection of potential muddles, again caused by similarities in sound.

a) What can I *wear* (i.e. clothing)? I need something new to *wear*.
b) *Where* (i.e. in what place) is the T.V. controller? It's not *where* I left it. Why can't people leave it *where* I put it? (This word always has a sense of place. One way to remember this is that it has the word *here* inside it!)
c) Why *were* (i.e. past tense of *are*) you so late? *Were* you at Naveen's house? We *were* worried about you.
d) *We're* (i.e. we are) feeling sick. *We're* going to the bathroom. *We're* never going to eat three bags of popcorn again.

Now try filling in the gaps:

W_____ going to have a party. W_____ both going to be eleven and Sarah and I _____ discussing it all through lunch with our friends. The two problems are _____ to have it and what to _____. I'd like to have it in the hall the disco was, as the lights _____ brilliant at Karim's party. W _____ having a meeting to discuss it later. Do you know _____ your high-heeled shoes are so that I can paint them yellow?

It would be helpful for Alice to make up some sentences of her own, using these words appropriately.

'Advice' and 'advise' sound different. This may help with similar pairs.

Practice, licence, advice

Spelling mistakes are common with these words – all nouns – as they are so like the verbs they are related to. So – Alice may have a piano **practice** – **a thing, a noun**, but she will **practise** – **a doing word, a verb**, the piano. Rajiv may *practise* his judo technique but he will go to a judo *practice*. *Licence* and *license* work the same way. Jyoti has a driving *licence* – a thing, a *noun*, but John is *licensed* to give professional advice and he sometimes has a drink in *licensed* premises – verbs. A helpful way to remember the difference is to think of *advice* and *advise* which also work the same way. John may seek *advice* – a *noun* – from Jyoti, who is a solicitor and she will *advise* – a *verb* – him. This one is easier because the two words – *advice* and *advise* – actually sound different. The 's' in *advise* is a softer sound. This may help you remember that the other verbs – *license* and *practise* – also have an 's' and not a 'c' in their ending! Alice and Rajiv could try filling in the gaps in this passage and John and Jyoti could make up other similar ones:

After football p_____ at school, Naveen rushes home to p_____ his ball skills. His father tries to a_____ him but Naveen doesn't want his dad's a_____. He prefers to watch his favourite Premiership video and get all the a_____ he wants from that. 'I get loads of p_____ at school,' he tells his dad, 'and loads of a_____ from my teacher!'

Effect and affect

This works similarly. Traffic fumes have a bad *effect* on Rajiv's asthma. They *affect* him adversely. **Effect is a noun and affect is a verb**. Alice and Rajiv could fill in the gaps in the following passage and John and Jyoti could make up their own as well:

'I don't think that late nights have a good _____ on your concentration,' said Sarah's mother after Sarah had fallen asleep over her homework.

'It's not the late nights that _____ me,' replied Sarah.

'It's the _____ of having to get up early in the mornings!'

(John and Jyoti will be aware that *effect* can also be used as a verb, e.g. in 'The bank manager told me that it would take a while to *effect* the transfer of funds into my account.' But this is a sophisticated usage and need not trouble Rajiv and Alice at present.)

To and too

This again tends to cause confusion in children who get anxious about writing correctly. John may need to help Alice understand that 'too' always has a sense of 'as well' or 'more than you need' – in other words, of the *muchness* of something e.g. 'Karim went and Naveen went *too*', or 'Karim ate *too* much pizza and Naveen was *too* full to finish his.' All other meanings which sound the same (except, of course, the number two!) will be spelled 'to' and don't have this sense of muchness, e.g. 'I go to school' or 'I am trying to finish this sum' or 'Can you tell me how to go to the station?'

Here is an exercise where the blanks can be filled in with either '*too*' or '*to*':

'We're going ___ have a picnic. Do you want ___ come ___?'

'Not much. What's there ___ do on a picnic? Anyway, I'm ___ tired and it's ___ wet. It's probably going ___ rain again, ___!'

'What a misery you are! Aren't you going ___ do anything today? Do come! I'm going ___ make a lovely picnic. Sarah and Laura are coming ___ and we may go the pond ___ hire a boat.'

'Oh all right! But I won't do anything ___ energetic. And I want ___ eat a lot ___. Understand?'
'___ right!'

Properly and probably

These two useful words – wholly different in meaning – can sound similar and confuse some children. Alice and Rajiv need to be clear which is which and also how each is spelled. John has certainly become accustomed to Alice's word 'probaly' which seems an amalgam of the two and many children do this until they practise the two words separately. It may be helpful to look at the following sentences and talk about their meanings – as well as the spellings! Then Alice will need to make up sentences of her own using each word appropriately.

Laura's little brother can't tie his shoelaces *properly*.
Do speak *properly*! I can't understand you when you mumble!
I want to play the piano *properly*.

We're *probably* going to Spain for our holiday.
It will *probably* stop raining soon.
If you really tried you could, very *probably*, pass this exam.

Except and accept

These two words also sound very alike and some children need help in knowing which is which when they have to write them. John needs to go over this with Alice and he can use the following exercise as well as some of his own. See how *except* and *accept* are used in the following sentences and then fill in the gaps in the passage below:

Everyone played cricket *except* Karim and Naveen.
Except for Geography, I like everything I do at school.

Laura cannot *accept* Sarah's invitation as she will be staying with her grandmother.

Naveen's brother said he was sorry for crashing the car but his parents would not *accept* his apology.

Everyone _____ Naveen came to Karim's party. His mother had telephoned to _____ the invitation but he didn't turn up. Karim refused to start the game without him. 'No-one _____ Naveen understands how to play,' he complained.

'I can't _____ that,' said Karim's dad. 'I can read the instructions and teach everyone else.'

'That would be fine,' said Karim, '_____ that you're holding them upside down.'

'Let's have tea,' suggested his mum.

'OK,' said Karim, 'we can eat everything _____ the twiglets because they're Naveen's favourite.'

Uninterested/disinterested

These two words, despite much popular usage, do *not* mean the same. An understanding of their distinct meanings is still worth having as, without such an understanding, an entire idea – as held in a word – will be lost. Although this book is not concerned to preserve out-dated uses, this one is worth fighting for and should be part of Alice's and Rajiv's basic education.

Uninterested – means, as you would suppose, having no interest in a subject, that it is boring, for example:

'I saw a programme on volcanoes which was supposed to be fascinating but I was totally *uninterested* in it.'
Or
'I tried to explain how my new invention works but the professor appeared to be *uninterested* in its possibilities.'

Disinterested – means something quite different. Look at the following examples:

'I don't bet on horses so my enthusiasm for racing is quite *disinterested*' i.e. Although I love watching races, I have no *financial interest* in the outcome. I can't gain from it.

'I'm not involved in politics so my enjoyment of the debates in the House of Commons is entirely *disinterested*', i.e. I won't gain, whoever wins. I just like the fun of the debating.

'When there was a lot of terrible fighting in Bosnia, the UN sent out *disinterested* observers so that they could get unbiased reports', i.e. the observers were not from one or other side in the fighting, had no personal interest in who won or lost, and so could be relied on for unbiased reporting.

It seems at this stage unnecessary to labour the point or to make too much of it with Rajiv and Alice. The chances are, though, that they will need *uninterested* and they may as well know that the above is the correct usage!

Less sugar but fewer lumps!

Fewer or less?
This again is a distinction worth preserving though it is becoming harder to do so!

The basic idea is that **fewer** is used when applied to **a number** of individual objects, e.g. people, shops, presents, biscuits etc. and **less** is used for **an amount** of something, e.g. meat, noise, water, money etc. A good way to remember the distinction is to think of *fewer* sugar lumps but *less* sugar. Another might be *fewer* bottles but *less* wine.

Alice could try putting the appropriate word in the blanks below (correct version on page 116):

Laura decided to invite her four best friends to dinner rather than have a birthday party this year. Her mother was pleased. '_____ friends means _____ mess,' she said. '_____ friends means _____ presents too,' replied Laura, ruefully.

'_____ spilled drink, _____ sausages trodden into the carpet, _____ crisp crumbs under the table, _____ waste paper and _____ tears when people don't win all the games. Sounds good to me,' mused Laura's mother. 'And _____ fun too,' thought Laura, beginning to change her mind.

Should have/should've

The problem here is not so much one of punctuation – this is dealt with below – it is to do with the way *should've* sounds. Perhaps not surprisingly, some children hear it as should *of* and then write it that way. Alice is one of these. She needs to *hear* it correctly and the following example may help if John can stress the italicised words:

'*Have* you done your homework?'
'No but I *should have*. I *should have* done my homework.'
'Where's Naveen? He *should have* been here ages ago.'
'*Has* he telephoned?'
'No, but he *should have*.'

The point is that Alice needs to *hear* that *have* is the essential word here – for the meaning of the sentence. This applies similarly when using *could have* and *would have* and elsewhere. She can now fill in the gaps using *should have*, *could have* or *would have* (correct version on page 116). She, could perhaps, then substitute these for the abbreviated versions, e.g. 'should've' for 'should have':

'I can't find my homework book,' said Karim.
'Could you have left it at school?' asked his mum, while

she was putting the shopping away.

'I _____ ____,' admitted Karim, 'but it _____ ____ been on the top of my desk and I _____ ____ seen it when I was packing my bag.'

'Well, you _____ ____ been more careful,' said Karim's mum. 'I _____ ____ thought you _____ ____ learned to remember important things by now.'

'I suppose I _____ ____ dropped it somewhere,' Karim wondered. 'Oh well, I'll have my chicken nuggets now and I'll ring Naveen about the homework afterwards.'

'Chicken!' shouted his mother. 'I knew I'd forgotten something!'

'Hm,' muttered Karim. 'I _____ ____ thought you ____ ____ learned to remember important things by now.'

Punctuation

Punctuation is essential for clarity but concern about it shouldnít inhibit free expression.

Punctuation matters. At its most important it can change, clarify or totally obscure the meaning of a sentence. However, some children at this stage get so concerned about the accuracy of their punctuation that, after half an hour's writing, they have managed only two lines of a story – having fretted far too much over getting the punctuation right. Important though punctuation is, John and Jyoti must ensure that concern about it does not inhibit Alice's and Rajiv's freedom of expression on paper.

One way to minimise concern is to help Alice and Rajiv understand what punctuation *is*, what it is *for* and *how it works*. It's quite simple when you know! Some adults spend all their lives nervous and unsure about correct punctuation and imagine it to be far more complicated than it is. The thought of apostrophes, for example, can reduce strong men to feeling like quaking ten-year-olds. Much better get it clear when you *are* ten!

Alice and Rajiv need to be able to use all the following with confidence: full stops, commas, capital letters, question marks, exclamation marks, hyphens, speech marks (quotation marks) and be able to organise and punctuate paragraphs and conversations. The finer points of colons, semi-colons, brackets etc. can wait at this stage.

   This book cannot offer a complete course in punctuation but, as with spelling, it provides help in identifying and remedying some of the more common problems. A number of practice passages follow in this section. Correct versions are given in Part Three but it is worth reminding John and Alice, as they embark on a punctuation blitz, that there is *always* more punctuation, such as commas and capital letters, to remember than they imagine. For example, in the first passage below, about Sarah and ballet, there are 33 corrections to be made!

Sentences and paragraphs

This was discussed in some detail above on pages 39–40. Alice may need reminding about the idea of a sentence being a container – a box – holding *one idea*. Each new idea needs a new box. Several boxes of connected ideas need a suitcase – a paragraph – to go in. She could practise on the following passage, writing it out, adding commas (7), full stops (10) and capital letters (15) where appropriate and deciding where she needs to start a new paragraph (1). John could first read the passage aloud, remind Alice not to start sentences with 'and' or 'but' and then see how she does. (They will find a corrected version of this and the other pieces that follow from page 116 onwards):

sarah has been going to ballet for years every thursday since she was four has been ballet class now she is bored and wants to try something else her friend laura is a brownie but sarah doesnt want to be a brownie karim does gymnastics but sarah thinks shes no good at gym naveen isnt sporty at all one day sarah has a new idea and tells her mother she wants to try judo her mother thinking this an excellent idea rushes out to buy a leotard sarah knows you need a special suit for judo they take the leotard back and come home with a judo kit

A good way to practise this is to copy out a passage from a book minus its punctuation and then for your child to write it out, putting the punctuation back in.

John may need to write out other comparable pieces for Alice if she isn't clear about what is needed here. (An easy way of doing this is just to copy a passage from a book, minus its punctuation.) When Alice is clear about sentences and full stops, she should have a go at breaking sentences into smaller sections, where appropriate, by using commas.

Commas

Children put them either everywhere or nowhere. Too often they are used where a full stop is more appropriate (see note on sentences as idea 'boxes' above). **They separate items in a list**, e.g. 'I bought apples, pears, bananas and grapes in the shop'. **In pairs they go round sections of a sentence** which could be taken out leaving the sentence still making sense, e.g. 'John, a hard-working father, makes time to help Alice, a clever girl, with her homework'. This sentence still makes sense if you take out the bits between the commas. (John may remember that these bits are *in parenthesis*.) Commas act as **pauses, after a short phrase**, e.g. 'Washing up, I noticed a crack in my favourite bowl'. There are examples of all these uses in the exercises below.

Alice could have a go at the following passage:

naveen a thoughtful boy really likes computers he also likes dinosaurs and modern reptiles but his best friend a boy called karim is more interested in football and other sports he is always trying to get naveen who hates sport to go to a match with him but naveen who dislikes noisy crowds prefers to spend a saturday afternoon on his computer with his other friends luke simon sahib and vijay

Punctuating conversation

This is usually the most problematic area for children of this age. There are a lot of things to remember in addition to the ones practised above and, for this reason, writing conversations should be a large part of John and Jyoti's work with their children. If we can assume that Alice and Rajiv are familiar with exclamation marks, question marks and their uses – even if they sometimes forget to use them! – we can concentrate on the more nerve-racking matters of indenting a line for a new speaker and the use of speech marks.

Speech marks and other things

Speech marks *enclose* speech. Anything that is *said* must have speech marks before and after it. This, in itself, is not a problem for most children – though many, having grandly opened speech marks at the start of a speech, forget to close them again. This is the first point to watch and check for. The second, and most frequent, problem with speech marks is that of forgetting to restart them again if a speech is interrupted by an 'asked Karim' or a 'Laura complained' in the middle of a sentence. For example:

> 'Why,' asked Karim, 'does it always rain on football days?'

Or:

> 'It's just not fair,' complained Laura, 'that everyone I know gets more pocket money than I do!'

The *speaking goes on* and needs speech marks to show that it does even if it is interrupted by narrative in this way. The example in the next paragraph shows how this works. The only way to master this is by *practising* and various suggestions for the writing of conversations follow later in this part.

If you open speech marks remember to close them again.

Starting a new line

During the course of a written conversation, if something is said by someone other than the last person who spoke, a new line – moved in slightly from the margin – is started. A new line, indented in this way, is always started when the speaker is anyone other than the last person who spoke. For example:

'Hi Karim!' called Naveen from the other side of the street. 'Where are you going? Somewhere interesting?'
'Oh sure,' replied Karim. 'Really interesting.'
'Well, tell me then!' his friend urged. 'It must be interesting if you're going in the opposite direction to school!'
'I'm going to see a really interesting chiropodist for my verruca,' said Karim. 'Like to come too?'

It's worth looking at any page of dialogue in a book to see how this works. Rajiv will be familiar with it but may not realise that he is.

In addition to speech marks before and after anything that is said, all speech must have some punctuation when it ends. If what is said is at the end of a sentence, e.g. 'Like to come too?', then it will end with a full stop, exclamation mark or question mark like any ordinary sentence. If, however, the sentence continues after what is said, e.g. '"Oh sure," replied Karim, crossly…' then the speech will end with a comma and the sentence will continue. Alice must train herself to remember that every speech, however short, will have some punctuation after it in addition to the speech marks. She could try to rewrite the following conversation, remembering all the above tools:

in the shops naveen met his friend karim karim was with his mum who is a friend of naveens mum the mums started talking at first naveen and karim did not mind then they got bored and karim who can be rather wild had an idea i am going to pile up all the cans of baked beans he said and i dare you to do it with the spaghetti hoops when the towers were higher than karim and naveen and about to topple over a shop assistant noticed what the boys had done the manager came over to the mums are these two boys with you he enquired watch out cried naveen the beans are falling over

Practice is everything with this kind of thing and Jyoti can set Rajiv any number of brief conversations to write. Popular subjects are:

Heard outside the staff room door
Left football boot to right football boot before or after the match
Before/after the party
Persuasions, e.g. Laura trying to persuade her parents to let her go to a sleepover/party/bowling/cinema/shopping centre etc.; Karim trying to persuade Naveen to come to a football match; Sarah trying to persuade her parents to give her a mobile phone/puppy/TV etc. for her birthday and so on.
Planning something
An argument
A confession

Apostrophes

Apostrophes do two totally different jobs. The *first* is to show where one or more letters have been left out, i.e. a word or words have been **abbreviated**, the *second* is to show that **something belongs to someone or something**. It is the second usage that causes most fear and trembling. As important as knowing where to put an apostrophe, is knowing where *not* to put one. *They*

Straightforward plurals do not need apostrophes!

emphatically are not needed in making plurals. Anxious writers spray apostrophes over everything and we find 'carrot's', 'tomato's', 'potato's' and so on, on display outside shops! Alice needs to understand that if no letters have been omitted in a word and if it isn't showing that something belongs to someone, e.g. 'Alice's book' then it does *not* need an apostrophe.

Apostrophes 1: abbreviations

'Should've', as explained above is a very good example of this. Other examples are: 'can't', 'won't', 'don't', 'I'm', 'you're', 'he's', 'she's', 'it's', 'we're', 'they're', 'I've', 'you've', 'we've', 'they've', 'I'd', 'you'd', 'he'd', 'she'd', 'it'd', 'we'd', 'they'd', 'isn't', 'wasn't', 'didn't', 'doesn't', 'couldn't', 'shouldn't', 'wouldn't' – and so on. There are many other uses of abbreviations of this kind, e.g. 'there's' for 'there is' or 'there has'. All these examples omit one or more letters and the apostrophe goes where the omitted letters would have been, e.g. in 'I'm', – the apostrophe is in the place of the 'a' from 'am' and, in 'can't', – the apostrophe is in the place of the 'no' from 'cannot'. ('Won't' is an oddity here!) This will all need careful practice but Alice should be assured that it is all entirely logical – she just needs to think what the 'long' version would be of anything she wants to write. She could start by going through the list in this paragraph, saying what the 'long' version of all the examples would be, e.g. 'I'm' would be 'I am'. Then she could practise on the following passage, abbreviating all the italicised words:

'*What is* the point of going to Naveen's house if *I am* not allowed to play in his tree house?' complained Karim. 'Naveen's *dad is* brilliant. *He has* made this amazing tree house. *It has* got all kinds of gadgets and doors and clever things like windows that really open and a ladder that unfolds on its own. *We are* really boring in this family and *there is* nothing to do and *dad is* no good at making things. *Ben is* going to help his dad make a table. *They have* got brilliant tools in their shed. Anyway, the tree house is really safe and *it is* the best tree house *I have* ever seen and *I will* be fine with Naveen's dad there, so, please Mum, say *you will* let me go!'

John could copy passages out of stories and write out the abbreviated words in full for Alice to re-abbreviate if she needs more practice. It is important that Alice puts the apostrophe in the right place. Teachers and examiners are unimpressed by apostrophes which hover hopefully over the middle of a letter!

Apostrophes 2: belonging

Most people think that this is much more complicated than it is. The basic rule is that *the apostrophe goes after the last letter of whoever or whatever the thing belongs to*, e.g. 'Laura's foot', 'Sarah's house', 'Naveen's school', 'Karim's mum'. In each case, the apostrophe has gone *after the last letter of whoever or whatever owns the thing* – if a mum is a thing! Here are some others: 'Mr Black's shop', 'Mrs Jones's office', 'Ms Singh's garden', 'James's house' – again, in each case, the apostrophe has gone after the last letter of the person to whom the thing belongs. Test these out for yourself – and the ones which follow. Here are some more: 'the girls' school' (i.e. the school belonging to the girls – note that as we don't say 'girl*ses*', no extra 's' is needed), 'the women's club' (i.e. the club belonging to the women), 'the children's playground' (i.e. the playground belonging to the children), 'the boys' football' (i.e. the football belonging to the boys), 'the girl's shoe' (i.e. the shoe belonging to the girl), 'the boy's game' (i.e. the game belonging to the boy). These should be studied very carefully to avoid any confusion about where the apostrophe goes. *It will be seen that the above rule applies,*

85

whether or not the original word ends with an 's' and whether it's singular or plural. It doesn't matter. We *add* an 's' as normal when a word ends with 's' and the sound demands it, e.g. in 'James's house' or 'Francis's bed', but, in 'the boys' club' – because we don't tend to say 'boy*ses*' – we don't. Either way, the apostrophe still always goes after the last letter of the person who owns the thing!

Alice can practise by turning these phrases round (the correct versions are on page 117), for example – the hat of the lady ➔ the lady's hat:

the homework of Sarah ➔ _____

the gym of the school ➔ _____

the cages of the animals ➔ _____

the staff-room of the teachers ➔ _____

the job of Mrs Watson ➔ _____

the car of Mr Das ➔ _____

the picnic of the families ➔ _____

the ideas of the professors ➔ _____

the speech of the president ➔ _____

the homes of the millionaire ➔ _____

the club of the men ➔ _____

the T-shirt of Thomas ➔ _____

Apostrophes – a final word

It is worth repeating, for those over-careful children who put in an apostrophe every time they see an 's', that it is only in these two cases – of *omitting a letter* or to show that *something belongs to someone*, that they are needed. They are *never* needed in words such as 'wants', 'likes', 'runs' – and so on, i.e. **ordinary verbs**. Rajiv may need practice in *stopping* putting them in such words! Likewise, it's worth repeating that they are *not* needed in **ordinary plurals**, e.g. 'horses', 'puddings' 'trees' and so on. Again, Rajiv may need this drawn to his attention in order to stop putting in unnecessary apostrophes.

Apostrophes are needed to show belonging or to show that letters have been left out. Nowhere else!

It's/its

These need a word of clarification. If something belongs to 'it', e.g 'the giraffe bent its neck' – in this case, we do not add an apostrophe to show belonging. This is to distinguish 'its' from 'it's', i.e. the abbreviated form of 'it is'. It may help to reflect that this works like 'his' – no-one would put an apostrophe in 'his'!

Its = *belonging to it*, e.g. 'the dog wags *its* tail', 'my car's lost *its* bumper', 'the spider made *its* web'

It's = *it is* or *it has*, e.g. '*it's* a lovely day', '*it's* my dog', '*it's* got a new computer room'

You're/your

This causes similar problems. Alice may need to think about the difference in meaning between the two.

Your = *belonging to you*, e.g. '*your* book ', '*your* house', '*your* friend' and so on

You're = *you are*, e.g. '*you're* a bit late', '*you're* coming too', '*you're* my best friend'

When Alice has got these right and understands the principles of the points explained above, it will be time for her to work through the following passages. These are unpunctuated and, in order for her to punctuate them correctly, she will need to have understood the points in the preceding pages and be able to use all the tools explained above.

Having said all this, it is important for John – and Alice – to accept that correct punctuation is not the most important thing in the world and anxiety about it must not in any way cramp Alice's ability to express herself freely and imaginatively on the page. All sensible teachers would rather see a page of free and imaginative writing than two perfectly punctuated, but nervily restrained, sentences. Too much time spent on punctuation at this stage is not time well spent.

Practice pieces

Here are four short passages all of which need rewriting using capital letters, full stops, commas, indentation, speech marks, exclamation marks, question marks and apostrophes. John may need to read them aloud to Alice first, as it can be quite hard to make sense of unpunctuated passages without help (correct versions are given on page 118).

look at my cat said laura shes got things crawling on her fur ugh screamed lauras mother whats the matter with her its disgusting what is it ive no idea mumbled lauras dad from behind his sons rice krispies packet who cares anyway sneered lauras brother paul a very tiresome boy cats stink its probably got fleas my friends sisters cat had fleas the size of gerbils

mr sloppys ice cream is declared sarah the best in the world rubbish replied naveen rudely my mums is loads better its made from real fruit so what said sarah mr sloppys couldnt be better lets see said naveen why dont we test them both on karim and laura and see whos right im right youll see retorted sarah nobodys better than mr sloppy and i should know because hes my dad

wheres my jacket yelled karims sister shireen from her room im late at the stables and its my turn to do the horses food theyll be starving its probably under your bed where i found your T-shirt socks sweatshirt and most of your underwear replied her overworked mum thanks mum shouted shireen but i cant find my jodhpurs thats the second pair this term sighed her mum despairingly i cant help it responded shireen jodhpurs arent cool anyway and mum dont get a shock when you come in but ive had my head shaved we live in altrincham part of greater manchester in cheshire so we live in england but we also live in great britain the british isles and in the united kingdom its a bit complicated were also part of europe the british commonwealth which used to be the empire and we also live in the northern hemisphere sometimes its said that we live in the west but i dont understand this we might be west of europe but we are east of the united states so it doesnt mean anything it all depends on where you are

Hyphens

Finally, a word about these little dashes. They are used when there is insufficient room to write an entire word on a line and it is necessary to break the word in two. Ideally, Rajiv and Alice should see the problem coming and begin the word on a new line, even if it means leaving a little more unused space than usual on the line above. However, if it is a long word and it is begun on the first line and needs to be broken, then care should be taken to break the word at a point when it breaks into its separate bits of meaning or when its sound breaks, e.g. 'break-fast' rather than 'brea-kfast' and 'light-ning rather than 'lig-htning'. However, a grasp of this tends to come with maturity and it should not be fretted over.

Writing Skills

In Part One of this book, John and Jyoti met various techniques and exercises for improving their children's writing skills and confidence. Here are some additional suggestions to help them to help Rajiv and Alice with those aspects of written work with which they need further practice. It is worth repeating that merely working through these exercises without having taken in the points and techniques explained in Part One will be of limited value.

The Blob from Mars revisited

You will remember that The Blob is useful as the recipient of clear descriptions of simple objects and their uses. This provides excellent writing practice, especially for children who find difficulty with writing clear descriptions or explanations, or with writing comprehensible consecutive sentences. Here is a list – some were given in Part One – of possible things to explain or describe to The Blob. You can also think up your own – though keep them simple!

bed	door	rake
belt	flower-pot	ruler
bottle	fork	shoe
brush	hammer	skateboard
button	knife	skipping rope
candle	mug	spoon
chair	needle	table
coin	pencil	watering can
comb	plate	yo-yo

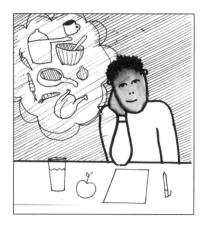

Descriptions and instructions

Rajiv and Alice could also just practise describing real objects as precisely as they can. This is good practice for vocabulary. For example, everyone knows what a lemon is but it is not easy to describe one in terms of texture, shape, smell, taste and so on. This could be tried with other fruits and other foods, e.g. an egg, a slice of bread, a chocolate bar, a cornflake, butter, yoghurt etc. This could become a game. For example, Rajiv could describe, say, a banana, and Jyoti has to guess, from his description, what the object is. This really does stretch and develop vocabulary and is a game the whole family can join in.

Making up *recipes* is a useful tool here. Rajiv could

either describe how to make a real recipe – giving the ingredients, the quantities, the method and so on or he could make up imaginary recipes – or *spells* – for things such as:

Getting Homework Done Quickly
Polishing School Shoes
Making a Horrible Teacher Invisible
Turning My Football Boots into Goal Scorers and so on.

Jyoti will know what sort of recipes will appeal to Rajiv! This is a useful exercise because accuracy of description is important in all recipes – real or imaginary – and clear, comprehensible description and instructions are necessary too.

The Beetle in the Fridge and the Spider in the Corner

These are two further exercises to help with clear and detailed description and the stretching of both the imagination and the vocabulary.

John could ask Alice to imagine the experience of a beetle stranded in their family fridge. The beetle has to negotiate its way around, perhaps, bread, eggs, milk, cheese, cream, vegetables, fruit and other ordinary things. But what would these things *feel like* for a beetle? What hazards might there be? If you were a beetle, how would it feel to slide down a large, free range egg into a jug of cream, for example? Alice can write about this from the beetle's point of view – but the emphasis is on detail.

Jyoti could ask Rajiv to imagine that a spider has made its web in a top corner of his room. What could it see from there? Is its view obscured by a cupboard? a chest of drawers? What does his bed look like from up there? What does it look like when the door opens? What does the spider understand of what it sees? What does it hear? feel? in that corner? Has it any food? Rajiv could write about

Looking at things from unfamiliar angles can make for unusual and detailed writing.

his own room from the spider's point of view and, again, the emphasis is on detail. This approach can be used in various contexts, e.g. the spider's view of the classroom, an insect's view of your garden, a bee is trapped inside your car and so on.

Under my bed

This is an excellent exercise and allows a child to develop all the techniques described above. The only problem is when a child has a bed which sits directly on the floor as some do. It is open to at least two possible approaches:

Alice wrote realistically about the mess under her bed – forgotten toys, outgrown slippers, sweet-papers, bits of fluff, magazines and so on – in detail. It was a factual, but well-detailed description. She could have written it from the point of view of an intrepid visitor – spiders are often useful! – to get a very different perspective of the nature or on the size of the various objects and this might have been more fun.

Rajiv wrote a piece of fantasy about an imaginary world under his bed – a world of small gnome-like people and their battle against the local enemy (from under his brother, Sanjay's, bed). It was pure fantasy and highly enjoyable. The title allows for this kind of freedom but also encourages clear description. Further suggested titles for writing follow.

Essay titles

These are a mixture of pure story-telling titles, descriptions, instructions, discussions and many that can be taken in more ways than one. Most of them would be fine as titles for timed essay work but Rajiv and Alice need to be reminded that essays on some subjects are easier to plan and complete within, say, thirty or forty minutes, than others. Timed essay practice is very important if Rajiv is going to sit entrance examinations.

Jyoti will need to give Rajiv plenty of practice in writing the various types of essay before the exams and this will also be of help to Alice before the move to senior school. The first set of titles below could be warm-ups for, maybe, 15 minutes.

Warm-ups
Describe carefully how you would:

a) pump up a bicycle tyre
b) cook a light meal, e.g. an omelette, cheese on toast etc.
c) re-wire a plug
d) wash a car
e) lay a table for a grand meal
f) make a costume for a play or a dance show
g) sew on a button
h) tie shoelaces
i) iron a shirt
j) plant a bulb
k) clean out a cage or a tank
l) groom an animal
m) make a bed
n) vacuum clean your room

Other titles
Allow 30–60 minutes for these – cutting down on the time as exams loom nearer and as Rajiv and Alice become more confident. They should be in sight of a clock while they work.

The Escape
*What I don't want to be
    when I grow up*
*Why I do/don't think
    television is a good thing*

Lost on the Underground
The Mysterious Chair
*My Life in 2005
    (6/7/10/30 …. etc!)*
The Coach Trip

The Party
The Best/Worst Present
A Terrible Fight
Lost Dog
The Storm
Flying
Swimming
Under the Pavement
The day I Drove a Bus
The Shed
An old building or old object
A job I would like to do
Children should never be
  smacked – do you agree?
The Ancient Tree
The Junk Shop
Visiting
The New Headmaster
If I had my own shop
The Key
The Magic Paint-box
Questions I should like to ask
My Favourite Shop
The Spotted Gringehopper
The Nightmare Journey
A Place I Know Well – detail!
A Day in the Country
A Walk in the Woods

Lost Guinea Pig
Trapped
The Race
Going Shopping
Why I would (not) like to be
  an Only Child
The Day I Climbed to the Top
Going for a Drive
Trick or Treat
The Prisoner
My Grandmother
A Visit to a Farm
Lost in a Crowd
A Very Unusual Teacher
Dancing
A Horrible Dream
A School Trip
My Favourite Food
The Repair Man
If I were Prime Minister for
  a day
Broken Glass
Dangerous Journey
My Hero
The Loch Ness Monster
The New House
My New Machine
A Visit to the Zoo Your friend

Nicky is about to come to your school. Write a letter to Nicky saying what you like and don't like about it. Would you recommend it?

You have to write a brochure about a place you like to visit (e.g. the zoo, leisure centre, park, theme park.) Describe it in detail making it sound as attractive as possible.

Letters and conversations

Two other approaches are letters to individuals, e.g. thank-you letters, fan letters, letters to newspapers on a particular topic, letters to a TV programme and so on. It is important that Alice and Rajiv know how such letters are set out and the differences between thanking Auntie Louise for the book-token and asking Blue Peter to do a programme on hang-gliding. It can be helpful to look at the letters page in a newspaper or magazine to get the idea. Conversations were dealt with in detail above, especially from the point of view of their punctuation. Rajiv and Alice might like to conduct imaginary – or real! – interviews with people in whom they are interested. This would involve writing down the questions beforehand and then transcribing, if the interview is real, or making up, if it is imagined, the answers. Grandparents make excellent interviewees and often children are fascinated by what they can learn about their relations in this context!

You would not write to your pen-friend in the same way that you would to a pop star or sports star or to your MP.

Continuations

Another frequently used method is to give Alice and Rajiv the start of a story which they then have to continue. This sort of question is quite common in entrance exams. Here are a few examples but you can think up your own:

a) I slammed the door of my room and threw myself onto my bed. I would have to do something and fast...

b) I had never before broken a promise. This time, however, I had no choice...

c) I had been swimming for several hours after the ship went down and was getting very tired when, suddenly, I saw land...

d) There it was again. The creaking that had woken me up. And was that a light under the door...?

Finally:

Have you remembered your postcard collection? If you have been conscientiously hoarding postcards, as was suggested back on page 19, you should by now have quite a collection. Alice and Rajiv will enjoy choosing one from a selection of 3 or 4 to write about – either as a description or a story.

Postscript – parts of speech

Alice and Rajiv will not need to know, at this stage, about grammar – parts of speech and so on, that is, unless the school of your choice tells you that this is required for the examination. However, it may be helpful for John and Jyoti to have their own recollection of these things polished up a bit. Here is a list of the principal parts of speech with a few examples:

Nouns

cat, house, school, spoon, sausage (common nouns)
Laura, Birmingham, Africa, Mr Blair, Eton College (proper nouns)
kindness, light, warmth, fear, size (abstract nouns)
herd, group, swarm, flock, team (collective nouns)

Adjectives

pretty, slow, heavy, noisy, hungry, difficult, clever, sleepy, quick, distant

Verbs

sit, walked, ate, thought, will work, wrote, speak, jumped, discuss, love, hate, read, learn

Adverbs

slowly, fast, madly, beautifully, well, late, heavily, often

Pronouns
he, she, I, you, we, they, them, us, me, him, her

Prepositions
in, under, between, through, at, for, with, to, after, off, on,
over, beside, beyond

Conjunctions
and, but, because, although, however

Articles
a/an (the indefinite article)
the (the definite article)

PART THREE

Introduction

This part is divided into two sections. In Section One you will find six comprehension exercises. These progress in difficulty from one to six. For further practice, you will need to raid a good bookshop. Collections of similar papers for 10–11 year-olds are readily available but, before you and your child work through any more, it would be wise to master the techniques discussed on pages 24–29 and practised here. One multiple choice comprehension paper follows. A few schools do examine in this way and Rajiv will need to have seen a sample of this kind of paper in order not to be surprised when he sits the exam. The passages are exactly the same but written answers are not required. As with ordinary comprehension papers, collections of these are available in bookshops. Finally, you will see an example of an entire paper – comprehension and essay – so that you have a fair idea of what to expect. It is, of course, entirely up to any individual school how they choose to examine and this is only one possible – though popular – model.

Section Two consists of correct versions of the exercises in Part Two of this book and a list deriving from work in Part One. Section Three consists of answers and discussions of the papers in Section One. Finally, there is an Afterword consisting of a model for a programme of work that you can adapt to your own needs. After that, you're on your own!

Section One

In all these exercises, Rajiv should be reminded to *read the passage carefully* before looking at the questions, to *answer as fully as possible*, to *leave a line* after each answer, to *check* over his answers and to take into account the *relative values in terms of marks* for the questions. It is silly to spend ten minutes on a question worth two marks and not have time for a question worth four! Most answers do require *full sentences*. He should also be reminded that he should attempt to *put down something* for each answer. A blank space cannot get a mark and it is worth the risk of being wrong to write down something – and it might be right! Suggested time limits are given at the end but these are only guidelines and you should not worry, at least in the early practices, if your child takes a little longer. If he or she finishes early, every minute should be used to make the answers as good, full and as accurate as possible! Check!

1. Banana Man

In 1878, the 2nd Lord Leconfield of Petworth House in West Sussex, sent his gardener to Kew to learn how to grow a banana tree. He had been told that bananas tasted better straight from the tree. All the necessary *paraphernalia*, including a special greenhouse, was installed at Petworth. What followed is recounted by his grandson:

"The banana tree was splendid. My grandfather took a lively interest in its progress until, lo and behold, it *fructified*. 'I will have that banana for dinner tonight,' he said, as soon as the banana was ripe. And so he did – amid a deathly hush. All were agog.

The banana was brought in on a *lordly* dish. My grandfather peeled it with a golden knife. He then cut a sliver off and, with a golden fork, put it in his mouth and carefully tasted it. Whereupon he flung dish, plate, knife, fork and banana onto the floor and shouted, 'Oh God, it tastes just like any other damn banana!' Banana tree and all were ordered to be destroyed. My famous old gardener told me that the banana cost my grandfather some £3000."

National Trust Magazine Summer 1998

Questions

1. Who was sent to Kew to learn about growing bananas?   1
2. Why did Lord Leconfield want a banana tree?   2
3. 'My grandfather took a lively interest' in the tree, says the writer. How might he have done this and why?   3
4. What was the atmosphere like as Lord Leconfield began to eat the banana? Try and describe it in some detail.   3
5. What happened when he tasted the banana?   3
6. Why does the writer say that the banana 'cost my grandfather some £3000.' What might have made it so expensive?   3
7. What do you think the following words mean? They are printed in italics in the passage:
   a) paraphernalia   2
   b) fructified   2
   c) lordly   2
8. What sort of man do you think Lord Leconfield was?   4

(25 minutes)   25

2. Pinched Legs!

Whoo! Emil jumped. He had nearly fallen asleep, and that would never do. He wished someone else would get in, so that he would not be alone with Bowler-hat, but no-one did, though the train stopped at several stations. It was still only four o'clock, so there was more than two hours to go before they reached Berlin. He tried pinching his legs, as that always helped to keep him awake during history lessons at school. Then he began to wonder what his cousin Pony looked like now, for he could not really remember her face at all. He only knew that when Grandma and Aunt Martha had brought her to Neustadt – oh, a long time ago – Pony had wanted to fight him. Of course he had refused. She was no more than flyweight then, to his welterweight, so it would have been quite unfair, and he had told her so. Why if he'd given her one of his uppercuts, they'd have had to scrape what was left of her off the wall! But she had kept on and on about it, until her mother got tired of it, and made her stop.

Ough! He was nodding again, and had nearly rolled off the seat. He pinched himself and dug his fingers into his legs until he was sure they must be black and blue, but it didn't seem to do a bit of good. He tried counting the buttons on the seat opposite. Counted one way there were twenty-four, counted the other, he could not make more than twenty-three. He leaned back, wondering why that was – and so fell sound asleep.

Emil and The Detectives, Erich Kästner

Questions
1. Where is Emil during this passage?   2
2. Why did he 'jump' in the first sentence?   2
3. Why did Emil hope someone else would get in?   2
4. Does Emil enjoy his history lessons? How do you know?   3
5. Why do you think Emil had refused to fight Pony?   3
6. Give two methods Emil uses to try to avoid falling asleep.   2
7. Can you think up any other things he might have tried?
   You will need at least two.   4
8. Write a paragraph about a time when you:
   a) tried to keep awake. Or: b) tried to fall asleep.
   You should write at least five lines. $\frac{7}{25}$

(30 minutes)

3. Buffalo Halt

After lunch, Mr Fogg, Mrs Aouda and their companions went back to their comfortable seats in the carriage and settled down to watch the varied scenery that passed before their eyes – vast prairies, mountains outlined against the horizon, creeks tumbling and foaming on their way. Sometimes, a great herd of buffalo would gather in the distance, looking like a moving dam. Huge armies of these ruminants* frequently pose an insurmountable barrier to the progress of a train on its journey. One can watch the animals in their thousands filing past in serried ranks for hours and hours, across the railway tracks. The engine is forced to stop and wait till the line is clear again.

That is exactly what happened on this occasion. At about three o'clock in the afternoon, a herd of ten or twelve thousand buffalo blocked the line. After slowing down, the engine driver tried to push his buffers through the side of the immense column of animals but he had to stop in the face of this impenetrable mass.

Everyone watched as the ruminants* marched peacefully by, occasionally bellowing noisily. They were larger than European bulls but had short legs and short tails, widely spaced horns and long manes which covered their muscular humps. There was no point in trying to stop such a migration. When buffaloes have set off in a particular direction, nothing can divert them or get them to change their course. They are a torrent of living flesh which no dam can hold back.

The travellers watched this curious sight from the platforms. But the one to whom the loss of time was most serious, Mr Phileas Fogg, stayed in his seat and waited philosophically till the buffaloes should be pleased to move out of the way. Passepartout was furious at the delay caused by this great collection of animals and was eager to take shots at them with his arsenal of revolvers.

'What a country!' he exclaimed, 'where mere cows can stop trains and plod along in a procession, not remotely hurrying themselves, and not caring in the least that they are stopping the traffic! For goodness sake! I should very much like to know whether Mr Fogg made provision for this hold-up in his schedule! And what a useless engine driver who hasn't got the nerve to drive his engine through these obstructive beasts!'

The engine driver certainly hadn't attempted to drive through the obstruction and had behaved very sensibly. The buffers would, no doubt, have crushed the first buffaloes but, powerful though it was, the engine would have had to stop eventually, the train would have been derailed and would have been left lying helpless by the wayside.

The only thing to do was to wait patiently and hope to make up the lost time by greater acceleration as soon they could restart the train. The buffaloes' march-past lasted three long hours and it was nightfall by the time the line was clear again. At the moment when the last of the herd were crossing the rails, the first were disappearing over the horizon.

Around the World in Eighty Days, Jules Verne

* ruminants are hoofed animals which live by chewing their food over and over again

Questions

1. Where are Mr Fogg and Mrs Aouda sitting at the start
   of the passage?   2
2. Explain how the 'varied scenery …. passed before their eyes'.   3
3. What problem is caused by the herd of buffalo?   2
4. Why was there no point in trying to stop the migration?   2
5. What is surprising about Mr Fogg's reaction? Why is it surprising?   3
6. What sort of person might Passepartout be?   3
7. In what way do you think the engine driver behaved 'very sensibly'?   3
8. Was the time spent waiting for the buffaloes lost forever or
   was there something the driver could do?   2
9. Describe in your own words and as fully as possible what the
   passengers could see after their long wait was nearly over.   <u>5</u>

(35 minutes)   <u>25</u>

4. Life on Earth

The world must have seemed a very strange, empty place when the dinosaurs had all gone. There were no other giant animals to take their place right away. The forests and plains would have seemed very quiet. There were no flying pterosaurs, or ichthyosaurs and plesiosaurs in the sea.

If you looked a little closer, though, you would have seen many animals still alive. There were birds in the trees, crocodiles and turtles in the rivers and seas, frogs, lizards, snakes, and small furry animals on the ground.

These furry animals were the mammals which had been around since Late Triassic times. The mammals lived beneath the feet of the dinosaurs, but they were quite small, generally no bigger than a mouse or a rat. During the Cretaceous period, some of the mammals became larger, reaching the size of a cat, but they could never become really large because the dinosaurs were around. When the dinosaurs had gone, the mammals had their chance. In the first 10 million years of the Tertiary period, which came after the Cretaceous, many new kinds of mammals appeared, like the first horses, bats, and large plant-eaters.

The forests filled up rapidly. The early horses, and their relatives, were about the size of terriers, and they fed on leaves. There were cat-like meat-eaters which fed on them. In the trees above were climbing, insect-eating mammals, some of which were the earliest relatives of monkeys and apes (and, of course, of humans).

On the open ground were some large plant-eating mammals, which were 4 metres (13 feet) long, and 2 metres ($6\frac{1}{2}$ feet) tall at the shoulders. Some of these forms had horns. It had not taken long before the mammals replaced the dinosaurs!

By about 25 million years ago, in the middle of the Tertiary period, many new forms of mammals had come on the scene: rabbits, elephants, camels, dogs, bears, pigs and beavers. A big change had also taken place in the long-necked camels. The largest plant-eaters were brontotheres and rhinoceroses. One of the rhinoceroses reached a length of 8 metres (16 feet) and a height of 5 metres ($16\frac{1}{2}$ feet – just like a dinosaur!) Brontotherium looked rather like a rhinoceros, but it had a strange double horn on its nose which looked like a catapult.

The Hamlyn Book of Dinosaurs, Michael Benton

Questions

1. The world 'must have seemed a very strange, empty place when the dinosaurs had all gone,' we are told in the first paragraph. In what three different ways would this have been noticeable?   3
2. Was the world really empty? How do you know?   2
3. What type of animal developed in new ways after the disappearance of the dinosaurs?   2
4. In paragraph 4, three different kinds of animal diets are mentioned. What are they?   3
5. Where did the largest animals live during the Tertiary period?   2
6. What did our own earliest ancestors eat?   2
7. What four facts can you find about a Brontothere ?   4
8. Three different pre-historic periods are mentioned in the passage. Find them and write them down in the order in which they occurred in real life.   3

9. Many mammals are named in the passage. Give the names of as
   many as you can. $\frac{4}{25}$

(40 minutes)

5. Costume Drama

Eventually we reached the bay, spread out the rugs on the sand, arranged the food, placed the battalion of wine-bottles in a row in the shallows to keep cool, and the great moment had arrived. Amid much cheering Mother removed her housecoat and stood revealed in all her glory, clad in the bathing-costume which made her look, as Larry pointed out, like a sort of marine Albert Memorial. Roger behaved very well until he saw Mother wade into the shallow water in a slow and dignified manner. He then got terribly excited. He seemed to be under the impression that the bathing costume was some sort of sea monster that had enveloped Mother and was now about to carry her out to sea. Barking wildly, he flung himself to the rescue, grabbed one of the frills dangling so plentifully round the edge of the costume, and tugged with all his strength in order to pull Mother back to safety. Mother, who had just remarked that she thought the water a little cold, suddenly found herself being pulled backwards. With a squeak of dismay, she lost her footing and sat down heavily in two feet of water, while Roger tugged so hard that a large section of the frill gave way. Elated by the fact that the enemy appeared to be disintegrating, Roger, growling encouragement to Mother, set to work to remove the rest of the offending monster from her person. We writhed on the sand, helpless with laughter, while Mother sat gasping in the shallows, making desperate attempts to regain her feet, beat Roger off, and retain at least a portion of her costume. Unfortunately, owing to the extreme thickness of the material from which the costume was constructed, the air was trapped inside; the effect of the water made it inflate like a balloon, and trying to keep this airship of frills and tucks under control added to Mother's difficulties. In the end it was Theodore who shooed Roger away and helped Mother to her feet. Eventually, after we had partaken of a glass of wine to celebrate and recover from what Larry referred to as Perseus's rescue of Andromeda, we went in to swim, and Mother sat discreetly in the shallows, while Roger crouched nearby, growling ominously at the costume as it bulged and fluttered round Mother's waist.

My Family and Other Animals, Gerald Durrell

Questions

1. Suggest two reasons why the family had gone to the bay.   2
2. What was 'the great moment'?   2
3. Why did Roger get 'terribly excited'?   2
4. What was 'the offending monster'?   2
5. Describe, as far as possible in your own words, Mother's costume.   3
6. What happened to the costume when Mother was sitting in the water?   2
7. Why do think it took so long for anyone to help Mother?   2
8. Imagine that you are Mother. Give your version of what happened
   to you during this extract.   5
9. Did you enjoy this passage? Explain why this piece of writing does or
   does not appeal to you, giving examples from the passage.   5
(40 minutes)   ___
                                                                            25

6. Mecca

From time immemorial, Mecca (or, as it is now often written, Makkah), has been a stopping place for travellers, maybe because of the well of Zamzam, which provided water in the mountainous desert landscape of western Arabia. At some time, a cube-shaped temple was built near the well. Muslim traditions connect its construction with Adam and relate that Abraham and his son Ishmael rebuilt it. This is the Ka'ba, the holiest shrine of Islam. Mecca attracted both worshippers and traders, and its position on a main trading route meant it enjoyed considerable prosperity. Until the seventh century C.E. (in the Christian Era), Arabs worshipped many gods – one creator of the universe, and a host of minor deities. This changed with the advent of Islam, when the Prophet Muhammad transformed Mecca into one of the greatest pilgrimage centres in the world.

Muhammad, the founder of Islam, born in about 570 C.E., was raised by his uncle, Abu Talib. He may have had early contact with Christianity on a trading journey to Syria. Married at twenty-five to Khadijah, a wealthy woman fifteen years his senior, he led a pious life. Later, in his forties, during a period devoted to meditation, he retreated alone to a cave on Mount Hira and spent time in prayer and fasting. Here, in a vision, an angel – whom he believed to be Gabriel – gave him the first verses of the *Qur'an*, the holy book of Islam. He was told to carry a message to the world that there was only one God, no others.

For three years, he only spoke of his beliefs in private. During this time, he is said to have received the verses of the *Qur'an*. Once he began to preach, Mecca became very hostile. In 622, Muhammad left for Yathrib (later Medina), narrowly avoiding death; this migration, or *hijra*, was the turning point in his life. Received with zeal, the number of his followers swelled.

In 629, Muhammad approached Mecca with 10,000 men, but met little resistance. His Muslim forces entered the city, casting out the idols that had been previously worshipped and initiating worship of the one God, Allah. The Prophet died in Medina in 632.

All over the world, around 900 million Muslims bow down to face Mecca at five different points during the day – at dawn, midday, afternoon, evening and night. In mosques, its direction is indicated by niches called *mihrabs*. Every year, in the month of *Dhu'l-Hijja* (the twelfth month of the Muslim calendar), pilgrims converge on Mecca from all parts of the world for the *hajj*, the great pilgrimage. All Muslims who possess the means must perform the pilgrimage to Mecca at least once in a lifetime. The city and its surrounding area are considered so sacred that non-Muslims are not admitted. With travel now much easier than in the past, over two million Muslims are able to make the pilgrimage to Mecca each year.

The Atlas of Holy Places and Sacred Sites, Colin Wilson

Questions

1. Why might Mecca have been important to travellers in ancient times? 2
2. In your own words, give two reasons why Mecca 'enjoyed considerable prosperity'. 4
3. How old was Khadijah when she married? Be careful! 1
4. What was the message Muhammad was given by the angel? 2
5. What was the reaction in Mecca when Muhammad began to preach? Can you explain why Muhammad's beliefs had such a strong effect? 5
6. What happened when Muhammad arrived in Medina? 2
7. How old was he when he arrived in Mecca with his army? 1
8. Why were the idols cast out? 2
9. How do Muslims in mosques all over the world know which way to face when they bow down to Mecca? 2
10. Explain in your own words what the *hajj* is and who makes it each year. $\frac{4}{25}$

(40 minutes)

7. Battle! (A multiple choice paper)

The Common and the streets leading up to it were the scene of our principal game.
It was played chiefly on Saturday, our whole holiday. We assembled, for example, at
the top of the road in the well-trodden garden of a doctor who had a rowdy son; each
bringing a weapon or several weapons, wooden swords and pikes, or daggers, shields,
pistols, bows, arrows and with horns and trumpets, and perhaps some bread and
cheese and an apple or orange. There sides were chosen. One side went out to seek a
fort in someone's garden or among the gorse bushes. Ten minutes later the other set
forth, often in two divisions. Sometimes **stealth** was the rule of expedition; we
advanced whispering and in some order. Sometimes everyone was shouting for his
own plans and against another's. At other times the methods alternated: the stealth
would become wearisome, we began to chatter and disagree; or the riot of anarchy
would suddenly strike us as wrong, everyone said 'hush", and for some minutes we
modelled ourselves on Sioux, Mohicans or Hurons★, crouching, pausing, trying to
hush the sound of our breathing. We forgot everything in this Indian ideal.
Nevertheless, the enemy had to be found. Nor were they loth. Someone was sure to
show himself and wave defiance, or to leap out on us, supposing we passed by. If seen
at a distance they might change the stronghold and there would be a chase. If they
were content to stand a storm, the second army would gather all its numbers together
and, with yells and counter-yells, batter and push them out or be battered and pushed
out itself. The struggle was one of character, not weapons. The side possessing the
fiercest and most stubborn boys won. The winners would then in turn fortify
themselves and sustain an attack; and so it went on, until a mealtime, or nightfall, or
rain, or a serious quarrel, finished the war.
The Childhood of Edward Thomas, E. Thomas

★Sioux, Mohicans and Hurons are the names of American Indian tribes

Questions
Each question has three possible answers. Underline the answer you consider to be the
correct one. Only underline ONE answer for each question.
1. The doctor's garden was:
    a) where the boys met
    b) where they had a battle
    c) where they kept their weapons   1
2. The second side waited ten minutes before setting out:

    a) to prepare their weapons

    b) to give the first side time to hide

    c) to eat their picnic   1

3. 'stealth' (in bold print in the passage) means:

    a) quiet and secret moving about

    b) taking things that belong to other people

    c) being well-organised   1

4. The main purpose of Side 2's expedition was:

    a) to escape the enemy

    b) to find Side 1

    c) to pretend to be Indians   1

5. Members of Side 1 sometimes:

    a) put out a flag

    b) blew on a trumpet

    c) jumped out to surprise them   1

6. If Side 1 stayed in the fort, there was usually:

    a) a terrible and dangerous fight

    b) a lot of noise and shoving

    c) a chase   1

7. 'The struggle was one of character, not weapons' means:

    a) the side which didn't use weapons won

    b) the side with the better weapons won

    c) the side with the stronger personalities won   1

8. The winning side:

    a) took over the fort

    b) continued attacking the defeated side

    c) had their own picnic   1

9. The passage describes:

    a) a game played roughly once a week

    b) a serious battle between two gangs on holidays

    c) a war between two sides always composed of the same boys   1

10. The most suitable title for this passage would be:

    a) My Childhood Memories

    b) Battles on the Common

    c) Cowboys and Indians $\frac{1}{10}$

(20 minutes)

Sample paper

Finally, here is an entire paper, in two halves – a comprehension and an essay. Rajiv should attempt this in 1¼ hours i.e. 45 minutes for the comprehension and 30 minutes for the essay. Any practice papers he tries after this should be done according to the specified time limit as it is important that he should be working within this by now.

Escape from the prison camp

Joseph is a prisoner. He is kept, chained, in a cell – a kind of large box on top of other similar boxes – in an outdoor prison called 'the cooler'.

On the evening of the third day the guard came as usual. When Joseph heard the soft thud of his footsteps in the snow, he crouched down on the floor at the back of his tiny cell. He had a smooth round stone and a catapult in his hands. He had made the catapult from pine twigs and the elastic sides of his boots. His eyes were fixed on the flap in the door. In a moment the guard would unlock it, peer inside and hand in the food.

Tensely, Joseph waited. He heard the key grate in the rusty lock of the outside door of 'the cooler'. The hinges creaked open. There was the sound of a match spluttering – the guard was lighting the lamp. Heavy boots clumped across the floor towards his cell.

Joseph drew back the elastic. He heard the padlock on the flap being unlocked. The flap slid aside.

The guard had not seen Joseph when the stone struck him in the middle of the forehead and knocked him down. The floor shook as he tumbled. He groaned and rolled over.

Joseph must act quickly, before the guard came to his senses. He knew the guard kept his bunch of keys in his greatcoat pocket. He must get hold of them without delay. He must lift the guard till they were within reach.

He took a hook and line from under his bed. He had made the line by cutting thin strips from his blanket and plaiting them together. The hook was a bent four-inch nail that he had smuggled in from his hut.

After several attempts, the hook caught in the top fastened button of the guard's greatcoat. He tugged at the line and drew the guard, still groaning, up towards him …. higher and higher.

Suddenly the line snapped. The guard fell back, striking his head sharply on the floor. The hook was lost.

Joseph had one spare hook, that was all.

He tried again. This time the cotton broke and the button went spinning across the floor.

He tried for the next button. Again the cotton broke.

He had begun to despair when he saw the keys. They were lying on the floor. They had been shaken out of the greatcoat pocket when the guard fell.

Quickly Joseph fished for the ring of keys and hauled it up. A few moments later he was kneeling beside the senseless body, hastily stripping off the uniform. There was no time to lose. Already the locking-up of the prisoners had started and he could hear the guards shouting at them outside.

Joseph felt warm in the guard's uniform. The greatcoat reached to his ankles. The fur cap had flaps for covering his ears. He smiled to himself as he locked the guard in the freezing cell. Then, turning up his collar so that the tips touched his cheek-bones, he went out into the bitter night.

He walked through the snow towards Block E, where the Hungarian and Rumanian prisoners were kept. In the dark shadows behind the huts he hid until the trumpet sounded the change of guard.

Hundreds of times he had watched the soldiers of the guard fall in and march out of camp. He had memorised every order, every movement. It seemed to him quite natural now to be lining up with the others.

'Anything to report?' the officer asked each of them in turn.

'All correct, sir,' they answered.

'All correct, sir,' said Joseph in his best German.

'Guard, dismiss!' said the officer.

Joseph dropped to the rear and followed the other soldiers out – out of the great spiked gate and into freedom. It seemed too good to be true.

Some of the soldiers stopped outside the guard-house to gossip. A few went in. Joseph walked straight ahead, turning his head away from the window light as he passed.

'Where are you going?' one of them called.

'Shangri La,' he muttered. It was the soldiers' name for the night club in the village where they sometimes spent their off-duty times.

Without looking behind him, he walked on.

The Silver Sword, Ian Serraillier

Questions

1. At what time of year did this incident happen? How do you know?   1
2. Why does Joseph wait 'tensely'?   1
3. In paragraph two, Joseph can't see anything but relies on
   what he can hear to know what is happening. Find three words
   which tell you what sounds he can hear.   3
4. Describe carefully and in detail how Joseph tried to get the
   keys from the guard.   4
5. Why did he strip the guard of his uniform?   2
6. How did Joseph know how to behave when lining up with the soldiers?   2
7. Was Joseph first through the gate? How do you know?   2
8. Why do you think he walked on, 'without looking behind him'?   2
9. What sort of a man do you think Joseph is? Back up your answer
   with evidence from the passage.   4
10. How does the writer build up suspense and excitement in
    this passage? Give as many examples as you can.   4
                                                        ‾‾
                                                        25

Essay

Answer ONE of the following:

   a) What do you think happens next? Continue the story from where the
      passage leaves off.

Or:

   b) Write a story called 'The Prisoner'.

Or:

   c) Write a story or a description in which the idea of disguise is an important part.

Or:

   d) Describe a place you found frightening.

(All marked out of 25 giving a total of marks out of 50 for the whole paper.)

Section Two

This section consists of correct versions and suggestions for the exercises in Part Two of this book and the lists of words promised on page 46 of Part One.

Part Two – Answers

Unscrambling
Football teams (from page 69)

Spurs	Liverpool	Aston Villa
Leeds	West Ham	Bolton
Chelsea	Arsenal	Burnley
Fulham	Blackburn	Newcastle

(from page 70)

Animals	**Colours**	**English Towns**	**Foods**
buffalo	yellow	Bristol	pizza
monkey	blue	Brighton	sausage
tiger	orange	London	bacon
lion	violet	Leeds	chips
giraffe	scarlet	York	salad
elephant	brown	Durham	cheese
crocodile	navy	Coventry	pasta
rabbit	green	Dover	curry
sheep	white	Lincoln	sandwich
wolf	grey	Norwich	cereal

Common confusions and mistakes

They're/there/their (from page 70)

Where are the boys? They're looking for their football. It went somewhere over there, in the bushes. They're probably crawling about on their hands and knees getting their trousers muddy. It's nearly dark now so there isn't much point carrying on looking. They're probably just enjoying getting dirty!

Wear/where/were/we're (from page 71)

We're going to have a party. We're both going to be eleven and Sarah and I were discussing it all through lunch with our friends. The two problems are where to have it and what to wear. I'd like to have it in the hall where the disco was, as the lights were brilliant at Karim's party. We're having a meeting to discuss it later. Do you know where your high-heeled shoes are so that I can paint them yellow?

Practice and advice (from page 72)

practice, practise, advise, advice, advice, practice, advice

Effect and affect (from page 72)

effect, affect, effect

To and too (from page 73)

to, to, too, to, too, too, to, too, to, to, too, to, to, too, to, too, too

Except and accept (from page 74)

except, accept, except, accept, except, except

Fewer and less (from page 77)

fewer, less, fewer, fewer, less, fewer, fewer, less, fewer, less

Should have/should've (from page 77)

could have, should have, would have, should have, would have, should have, could have, should have (would have is also acceptable), would have

Punctuation

(from page 79)

Sarah has been going to ballet for years. Every Thursday, since she was four, has been ballet class. Now she is bored and wants to try something else. Her friend, Laura, is a brownie but Sarah doesn't want to be a brownie. Karim does gymnastics but Sarah thinks she's no good at gym. Naveen isn't sporty at all.

One day, Sarah has a new idea and tells her mother she wants to try judo. Her mother, thinking this an excellent idea, rushes out to buy a leotard. Sarah knows you need a special suit for judo. They take the leotard back and come home with a judo kit.

(from page 80)

Naveen, a thoughtful boy, really likes computers. He also likes dinosaurs and modern reptiles but his best friend, a boy called Karim, is more interested in football and other sports. He is always trying to get Naveen, who hates sport, to go to a match with him but Naveen, who dislikes noisy crowds, prefers to spend a Saturday afternoon on his computer with his other friends, Luke, Simon, Sahib and Vijay.

(from page 82)

In the shops, Naveen met his friend, Karim. Karim was with his mum who is a friend of Naveen's mum. The mums started talking. At first, Naveen and Karim did not mind. Then they got bored and Karim, who can be rather wild, had an idea.

'I am going to pile up all the cans of baked beans,' he said, 'and I dare you to do it with the spaghetti hoops.'

When the towers were higher than Karim and Naveen and about to topple over, a shop assistant noticed what the boys had done. The manager came over to the mums.

'Are these two boys with you?' he enquired.

'Watch out!' cried Naveen. 'The beans are falling over!'

(from page 84

What's, I'm, dad's, He's, It's, We're, there's, dad's, Ben's, They've, it's, I've, I'll, you'll

(from page 86)

the homework of Sarah → Sarah's homework
the gym of the school → the school's gym
the cages of the animals → the animals' cages
the staff-room of the teachers → the teachers' staff-room
the job of Mrs Watson → Mrs Watson's job
the car of Mr Das → Mr Das's car
the picnic of the families → the families' picnic
the ideas of the professors → the professors' ideas
the speech of the president → the president's speech
the homes of the millionaire → the millionaire's homes
the club of the men → the men's club
the T-shirt of Thomas → Thomas's T-shirt

(from page 88)

'Look at my cat,' said Laura, 'she's got things crawling on her fur.'

'Ugh!' screamed Laura's mother. 'What's the matter with her? It's disgusting! What is it?'

'I've no idea,' mumbled Laura's dad from behind his son's Rice Krispies packet.

'Who cares anyway?' sneered Laura's brother, Paul, a very tiresome boy. 'Cats stink. It's probably got fleas. My friend's sister's cat had fleas the size of gerbils.'

(from page 88)

'Mr Sloppy's ice cream is,' declared Sarah, 'the best in the world.'

'Rubbish!' replied Naveen, rudely, 'my mum's is loads better. It's made from real fruit.'

'So what?' said Sarah. 'Mr Sloppy's couldn't be better.'

'Let's see,' said Naveen, 'why don't we test them both on Karim and Laura and see who's right?'

'I'm right, you'll see,' retorted Sarah. ' Nobody's better than Mr Sloppy and I should know because he's my Dad.'

(from page 88)

'Where's my jacket?' yelled Karim's sister, Shireen, from her room. 'I'm late at the stables and it's my turn to do the horses' food. They'll be starving!'

'It's probably under your bed where I found your T-shirt, socks, sweatshirt and most of your underwear,' replied her overworked Mum.

'Thanks, Mum,' shouted Shireen, 'but I can't find my jodhpurs.'

'That's the second pair this term,' sighed her Mum, despairingly.

'I can't help it,' responded Shireen. ' Jodhpurs aren't cool anyway and, Mum, don't get a shock when you come in, but I've had my head shaved.'

(from page 89)

We live in Altrincham, part of Greater Manchester in Cheshire, so we live in England but we also live in Great Britain, the British Isles and in the United Kingdom. It's a bit complicated. We're also part of Europe, the British Commonwealth, (which used to be the Empire) and we also live in the northern hemisphere. Sometimes it's said that we live in the West but I don't understand this. We might be west of Europe but we are east of the United States so it doesn't mean anything. It all depends on where you are.

Vocabulary

Finally, you may remember George and Helen (pages 44 and 45 in Part One).

Here are lists of words that you could substitute for 'said', in George's case, and 'went' in Helen's. There are a random 100 or so in each of these lists but there are at least as many more you could find in each case. Add your own to the lists.

'It's raining,' George _____ .

acknowledged	demanded	queried	snorted
allowed	exclaimed	questioned	sobbed
announced	explained	persevered	spat
answered	gasped	persisted	stammered
barked	granted	pleaded	stormed
bawled	grimaced	proclaimed	stuttered
bayed	groused	protested	suggested
bellowed	growled	purred	tittered
blasted	grumbled	rallied	trilled
brayed	grunted	ranted	triumphed
breathed	hinted	rasped	trumpeted
cackled	hissed	rejoined	ventured
called	hooted	replied	volunteered
carped	howled	reported	vouchsafed
cawed	insisted	responded	wept
cheeped	interrupted	retorted	wheezed
chirped	joked	roared	whimpered
chirruped	laughed	scolded	whined
chortled	lisped	screamed	whinged
chuckled	moaned	shouted	whinnied
claimed	mumbled	shrieked	whispered
complained	munched	sighed	whistled
coughed	murmured	smiled	yelled
cried	muttered	smirked	yelped
decided	neighed	snarled	
declared	niggled	sniffed	

Helen _____ up the hill.

advanced	escaped	proceeded	steamed
ambled	fled	processed	stormed
barged	flew	prowled	strayed
beetled	galloped	raced	strolled
belted	hared	ran	stumbled
bobbed	hiked	roved	swaggered
bounced	hopped	sauntered	swayed
cantered	idled	scampered	tacked
capered	jogged	scarpered	tiptoed
careered	journeyed	scrambled	trailed
charged	limped	shuffled	toddled
chugged	loitered	sidled	traipsed
climbed	loped	skipped	tramped
clumped	lumbered	skulked	travelled
continued	marched	slipped	tripped
crawled	meandered	slithered	trotted
crept	moved	sneaked	trudged
danced	paced	sped	trundled
darted	padded	splashed	vanished
dawdled	paraded	sprinted	vaulted
disappeared	plodded	staggered	waddled
dodged	plunged	stalked	waded
dragged	pottered	stamped	walked
drifted	pranced	started	wandered

Section Three

This section consists of guidelines and answers for the exercises and papers in Section One of Part Three. The answers given here are suggestions. Obviously, the factual content must be correct but the exact wording used will, of course, vary.

1. Banana Man

1. *The gardener was sent to Kew,* is sufficient.
2. *He had heard that bananas taste better straight from the tree,* is sufficient.
3. *He might have visited it and asked questions about it. This is because he was going to a lot of trouble and expense to grow it.*
4. *The onlookers were full of excitement and no-one dared say anything. Everyone watched in suspense* etc. The question is worth only 2 marks so much more is unnecessary unless there is time to spare.
5. *He flung the dish, the banana and his cutlery onto the floor in a rage, exclaiming that the banana tasted 'just like any damn banana.'* – or something close to this.
6. A good answer to this – given the number of available marks – will talk of the training of the gardener, the expensive building of the special greenhouse, the length of time the tree would have taken to grow and the final, wasteful destruction of it all.
7. Any reasonable equivalents that would make sense in the context would be acceptable here, e.g. a) *equipment, tools and necessary materials* b) *bore fruit, produced a banana* c) *grand, magnificent, richly ornate* etc.
8. Again, for 5 marks, this should be fairly detailed. Examiners would look for evidence of reading between the lines, e.g. *he is extravagant, given to sudden enthusiasms and wild ideas, unreasonable and bad-tempered, even childish,* and so on

2. Pinched Legs

1. *Emil is on a train,* is quite sufficient.
2. *He jumped because he had nearly fallen asleep and didn't want to,* is sufficient.
3. *He didn't want to be alone with 'Bowler-hat',* is sufficient.
4. This question needs both its parts answered. *No, Emil doesn't enjoy history lessons. I know this because he finds himself falling asleep during them.*
5. *He refused to fight Pony because, as she weighed less than him, it would have been unfair,* will do, but, as the question asks, 'why do you think...?' it would not be wrong –

though hardly politically correct! – to add a comment about her being a girl or suggesting that Emil felt he was much too powerful for her.

6. *He pinches his legs and he counts buttons on the seat.*

7. There are no right or wrong answers here – anything intelligent and imaginative in the context would gain marks.

8. The only danger here is in not obeying instructions, especially the *either/or* nature of the question.

3. Buffalo Halt

1. *They are in comfortable seats in their railway carriage/train.* 'In a train,' on its own is insufficient.

2. The skill here is in describing how a seated passenger sees what is passing on a train journey by looking through the window. This needs to be well-described to gain all marks.

3. *The buffalo pass across the railway line in a huge crowd, row on row, and block the line so that the train can't continue on its journey.*

4. *It is impossible to stop or divert a herd of buffalo once it has started off.*

5. Something that explains that *Mr Fogg was very pressed for time and would not have wanted this delay but that he seems very calm.*

6. *Passepartout seems to be an impatient and excitable person who would be happy to shoot at the buffalo and who is not prepared to make allowances for different customs in a foreign country.*

7. *As it would have been impossible to divert the herd and as he would probably just have damaged and even derailed his train, the driver did the right thing in just waiting till the herd had passed by.*

8. *The driver could go faster than planned (accelerate) to make up some of the time.*

9. This requires an understanding of the immensity of the herd and of the fact that it stretches from immediately in front of the train to way off on the horizon.

4. Life on Earth

1. The two crucial points here are that the answer must come from the first paragraph, as stipulated, and that it should mention the three 'empty' areas – the land, the sky and the sea.

2. The answer is in two parts: a) *no, the world wasn't empty* and b) *I know this because the second paragraph gives examples of the various animals which could be found.*

3. *Mammals developed in new ways,* is sufficient.

4. One mark for each diet: *leaves, meat, insects*.
5. *They lived on open ground*, is sufficient.
6. *They ate insects.*
7. Any four from a) *they were large* b) *they ate plants* c) *they were mammals* d) *they had horns* e) *they looked like rhinoceroses* f) *they lived on open ground*
8. *Triassic, Cretaceous, Tertiary*
9. *mouse, rat, cat, horse, bat, terrier, monkey, ape, human, rabbit, elephant, camel, dog, bear, pig, beaver, brontothere, rhinoceros* (1 mark for each 4)

5. Costume Drama

1. Two from – *The family went to swim, to sun-bathe, to have a picnic.*
2. *This was when mother stood up in her new costume and prepared to go into the water.*
3. *Roger thought Mother was being attacked by a sea-monster and he wanted to defend her.*
4. *This was the swimming costume.*
5. *The costume was large and very impressive. It seems to have been made of very thick material, was baggy, and had a lot of frills and fluttery, extra bits of material attached to it.*
6. *It expanded and took in a lot of air, blowing up like a balloon.*
7. *No-one was able to help Mother for so long because they were laughing too much.*
8. A good answer to this question would, first of all, include the various stages of the incident, e.g. the display of the costume and entering the cold water, the attack by Roger, the sitting down, Theodore's rescue and so on. It would also omit the unflattering descriptions of the costume. For full marks it would have to convey what it felt like to be Mother undergoing this experience – perhaps even the frustration with her unsympathetic family!
9. This is clearly an individual and subjective question. For full marks, there would need to be a real engagement with the passage and a use of it in detail to convey one's own feelings. For example – *I like the bit when the costume gets blown up as I can really imagine what this looks like…* or *I think the writer creates very believable characters in just a short passage.* It is, of course, possible that Rajiv doesn't like it but it is much harder to write critically at this level.

6. Mecca

1. *Mecca might have been important because of the well* is sufficient.
2. *Mecca attracted worshippers to the shrine as well as lots of traders. All these visitors would have helped to make it prosperous.*

3. *Khadijah was forty when she married.*

4. *The angel told Muhammad that there was only one God.*

5. *The reaction in Mecca when Muhammad began to preach was hostile/angry/cross/worried. This was because he wanted to change the religion and stop people worshipping the gods they were used to and turn to one single God – something* that gets across these facts is necessary here.

6. *People were very enthusiastic about him and he got many more followers.* This is a hard question because of the vocabulary involved.

7. *He was 59.*

8. *The idols were cast out because Muhammad and his followers wanted people to worship only one God and not lots of gods and idols.*

9. *Muslims who want to face Mecca know which way to turn when they are in mosques because there are niches which show the right direction.* This is not easy to explain and credit should be given for understanding the idea even if the expression isn't perfect.

10. *The* hajj *is a great pilgrimage which all Muslims who can should make at least once in their lives. Two million manage it each year.*

7. Battle !

The answers to this one should be straightforward, if the passage has been read with care, and the purpose of the exercise is really to familiarise Rajiv with the format.

1. The doctor's garden was: a) where the boys met
2. The second side waited ten minutes before setting out: b) to give the first side time to hide
3. 'stealth' means: a) quiet and secret moving about
4. The main purpose of Side 2's expedition was: b) to find Side 1
5. Members of Side 1 sometimes: c) jumped out to surprise them
6. If Side 1 stayed in the fort, there was usually: b) a lot of noise and shoving
7. 'The struggle was one of character, not weapons' means: c) the side with the stronger personalities won
8. The winning side: a) took over the fort
9. The passage describes: a) a game played roughly once a week
10. The most suitable title for this passage would be: b) Battles on the Common

8. Escape from the Prison Camp

1. *It happens in the winter. I know because Joseph hears the guard's footsteps in the snow.* Both parts of the answer are needed for the marks.

2. *He waits tensely because he is nervous and anxious, he doesn't know how things will turn out and because it is so important.* A good answer will convey this mix.

3. Any words not from paragraph two will be discounted. Any 3 from these are acceptable: *grate, creaked, spluttering, clumped.* Only 3 marks are available.

4. *Joseph used a catapult made of boot elastic and pine twigs to shoot a smooth round stone onto the forehead of the guard. This knocked him out. The guard kept the keys in his pocket. As the guard was lying there, Joseph dropped a hook on a line and tried to hook it into the guard's button to draw him up to where he could reach the pocket. However, the line broke twice and each time the guard fell back to the floor.* A good answer will use all this information. This amount of detail and clarity is necessary for full marks.

5. *Joseph needed to wear the uniform as a disguise so that soldiers would think he was one of them. It also kept him warm!* The first point is the one needed for the marks.

6. *He had seen the soldiers marching, lining up and obeying orders so often that he knew it all by heart and it was easy for him to do as they did.*

7. A good answer will pick up Joseph's *dropping 'to the rear'*, the word *'followed'* and explain what these imply.

8. *Joseph doesn't look behind him partly because he wants to look confident and partly because he doesn't want to risk being recognised.* This is the obvious answer but the question allows for other plausible responses.

9. This is an opportunity to read between the lines. Full marks go to an answer which conveys Joseph's foresight and resourcefulness (pine twigs, boot elastic, nail), his physical strength (lifting the guard), his tenacity, patience, bravery and nerve under stress – the whole episode. Some children may see him in a negative way – e.g. he is in prison so he must be bad, he hurts the guard and so on. However, best answers will refer to the passage as evidence of the characteristics they identify. At least three sentences will be needed here.

10. Best answers will write in detail about Joseph's tense wait, the protracted efforts to get the keys and the will-he/won't-he be caught nature of the end of the passage. There is lots to say!

Essay

The familiar criteria will be important here. If Rajiv has half an hour for this piece, about 200 words or more will be necessary. High marks will go to a well thought-out piece which is relevant to the title and, in the case of (a), plausible. Spelling and punctuation accuracy help but are not the most important thing. Ideally, Rajiv should have time at the end to check his entire paper and feel, as he hands it to Jyoti, that he has done himself justice and even enjoyed it!

Postscript

With luck, he will make it to the school of their choice. However, either way, they can be sure that, having worked through the principles and exercises in this book, he and Alice can look forward to a senior school experience for which, in terms of all work which relies on reading and writing, they are now far better prepared.

Afterword

Programme of work

Each Parent – Child partnership will need to identify those aspects of written work with which the child is already comfortable and which skills need work. The table below covers all the aspects of competence in English dealt with in the book and suggests a scheme of work. Every pair will need to navigate the scheme to suit their own priorities and needs – spending more time on some areas and less, or none, on others. The schemes for comprehension and essay work are given in parallel and, in some cases, are merged, as the same skills are needed in both areas. It is, in any case, sensible to work on both areas concurrently – not on comprehensions first and essays second, for example. This is partly for variety – wall-to-wall comprehension work is boring and constant essay practice can make for mechanical writing. It is also because, as pointed out above, the skills involved are identical and need to be developed together.

How to use this programme

Having read and discussed together the areas of work covered by Part One of the book, use this programme to map out your own scheme, giving priority to those aspects with which your child is least confident or which, during your assessment, seem most in need of help. Allow time for follow-up work. Few problems are solved with a single exercise or session. They will all need reinforcement, extra practice, reminders. Learning – or in some cases, unlearning, can be a slow process! Remember to stick to time limits. Don't let lessons overrun. Also, don't let timed practices overrun. It is important that exam candidates – and all children are, sadly perhaps, exam candidates in some ways – have a sense of working to a time limit, in order to do themselves justice.

Programme

Preparation

See pages 18–19 for what is needed. Be prepared before you start!

Assessment

COMPREHENSIONS: Preliminary exercises for assessment are suggested on pages 20–2.

ESSAYS: Suggestions for preparatory informal exercises are given on pages 22–3.

Dyslexia

If you have any concerns of this kind, consider the points on pages 55–6 and take any appropriate action at this stage.

Work

Having read through Parts One and Two of this book, you should be able to make your own programme of work based on your child's strengths and weaknesses. Think as flexibly as possible. You will need to be prepared for unforeseeables cropping up – interesting ideas or explorations or even problems which need following-up but which will take time. This is usually teaching at its most stimulating and best! Having said this, it is still important not to go over the time you allow for each session. Much better to have a child saying, 'can't we go on?' than 'when can we stop?'

COMPREHENSIONS: Study together the points on pages 24–9. This may result in some helpful discussion – depending on how much practice each child has already had at school. These points will also be worth remembering when the exercises later in the book are tackled.

ESSAYS: Read together the points on pages 29–36 and discuss them. Allow time to share thoughts and experiences about these suggestions. Each child will recognise himself or herself in some of the comments here.
Practise the exercises on pages 34–6.

Clarity and style

Exercises on pages 37–42 and 44–6. Spelling help on pages 52–5 and 61–75.
Punctuation help on pages 78–89.
Common mistakes on pages 70–8.
Each individual child will need to work on these points and exercises increasingly independently. Thereafter each pair will find it helpful to compare the results with the answers and explanations given on pages 115–18 and discuss any discrepancies.

Checking techniques

Read pages 46–52 and discuss which of these techniques will be of most help to your child. Some trial and practice may be useful to select the best method(s). Then, as a matter of course, *use* the chosen method *after every piece of work*.

COMPREHENSIONS: *Exercises* on pages 102–114 and *answers and explanations* given on pages 121–6.
These will need careful working through so that each child grasps the appropriate techniques.

ESSAYS: *Varieties of writing*, exercises on pages 89–95.
Parents can use these as examples and then make up their own.

Practice Paper

When you feel all skills have been practised sufficiently to allow your child to have gained maximum confidence, then have a go at the paper on page 112, sticking to the time limit. Doing it too early will undermine confidence and undo the useful work done hitherto. Whatever the result, praise, praise, praise!